The Ultimate Bug Out Bag Guide

Richard Lowe

The Writing King

The Ultimate Bug Out Bag Guide

Copyright © 2026 by Richard G. Lowe

Table of Contents

Prologue 6

Introduction 7

Chapter 1: Choosing Your Bug Out Bag 10

Chapter 2: Water and Hydration 16

Chapter 3: Food and Nutrition 23

Chapter 4: Power, Light, and Communication 30

Chapter 5: Shelter and Weather Protection.......................... 38

Chapter 6: Health and Hygiene 45

Chapter 7: Tools and Equipment............................... 53

Chapter 8: Documentation and Information 60

Chapter 9: Personal Security 68

Chapter 10: Special Considerations............................ 76

Chapter 11: Maintenance and Testing 92

Chapter 12: Multiple Bug Out Bag Strategy......................... 100

Chapter 13: When Minutes Matter 107

Chapter 14: Integration with Emergency Plans.................... 116

Chapter 15: When Staying Put Is the Answer 123

Chapter 16: What to Wear 130

Chapter 17: Cooking Systems.................................134

Chapter 18: Signaling and Being Found 138

Chapter 19: What to Carry on Your Person 142

Chapter 20: Your Vehicle as an Emergency Resource...........146

Chapter 21: The Medication Kit..................................152

Chapter 22: Building Your Kit on a Budget 160

Chapter 23: Firearms in Emergency Preparedness 163

Appendix: Complete Bug Out Bag Checklist 172

Conclusion 176

About the Author 178

Books by Richard Lowe..181

See books by Richard Lowe at

https://masterofworlds.com

Get free publishing insights and industry updates at

https://thewritingking.substack.com

For ghostwriting and book coaching services see

https://thewritingking.com

Prologue

At 4:31 AM on January 17, 1994, the Northridge earthquake threw me out of bed and changed everything I thought I knew about being prepared for emergencies.

I'd been hiking and camping for years. I had emergency supplies. I thought I understood disaster preparedness. But when the ground stopped shaking and we realized our son was missing, all that theoretical knowledge became worthless. We spent the next terrifying hours stumbling through a damaged city with no power, no phones, and no idea where to look for him.

That earthquake taught me the difference between having emergency gear and being prepared. It showed me that most emergency planning fails because it assumes you'll have time to think, time to gather supplies, and time to make careful decisions. Real disasters don't work that way. They hit fast, hit hard, and leave you dealing with chaos while making life-or-death decisions with whatever you can grab in the dark.

This book isn't about building the perfect survival kit or preparing for the apocalypse. It's about real emergency preparedness that works when you have minutes to evacuate, when your carefully laid plans fall apart, and when the only thing standing between your family and disaster is what you've prepared in advance.

Every recommendation in these pages comes from gear I've used, techniques I've practiced, or lessons learned the hard way during actual emergencies. Because when the ground starts shaking or the evacuation sirens start wailing, there's no time for theory. There's only what you know, what you have, and what you can do with both.

Your bug out bag might never save your life. But if the day comes when you need it, you'll want it to work.

Introduction

Understanding Emergency Evacuation

Disasters don't wait for convenient times. I learned this during the Northridge earthquake early in the morning. My wife and I were jolted awake by what felt like the world ending. The furniture in our apartment became possessed, dancing and sliding across the floor like something out of a horror movie. Our kitchen table moved six feet on its own, the refrigerator relocated itself to the other side of the room, and books turned into missiles flying off the shelves.

The real terror came when we realized our teenage son was missing. He'd left the house earlier with his headphones on, as teenagers do, and we had no idea where he was. My wife ran barefoot through the broken glass from our shattered dishes, cutting up her feet because we didn't even have a basic first aid kit. We spent twenty-four agonizing hours not knowing if our child was alive or dead. When we finally found him, he'd been stranded miles from home in downtown Hollywood when the power went out, with no way to contact us and only a few dollars in his pocket.

That experience taught me we were woefully unprepared for something that, living in Southern California, we should have expected. We had no emergency supplies, no communication plan, no first aid kit, and no idea what to do when disaster struck. We were just regular people living normal lives, assuming emergencies happened to other people.

That wasn't my only brush with disaster. A few years earlier, I was driving down the mountain from Lake Arrowhead to college when I suddenly realized the forest around me was on fire. Trees and shrubs were burning on both sides of the road, and when I looked back, I saw the fire had jumped the road behind me. I was trapped with fire in every direction, honestly thinking I was going to die. A firefighter ran up to my car, jumped in, and directed me to drive to a specific spot where a helicopter dumped water directly on us. That's the only reason I survived.

Then there was the Christmas hike in 1986 when my father and I decided to explore a beautiful canyon in the San Bernardino Mountains. What started as a simple morning hike turned into a nightmare when we got lost, my father had what appeared to be a heart attack, and I had to climb out of the canyon in the snow to get help. The fire department airlifted my father out the next day from a spot they named "Lowe's Meadow."

Why You Need a Bug Out Bag

These experiences, along with my twenty years managing disaster recovery for Trader Joe's, taught me that preparation isn't paranoia (it's practical common sense). The world has only become more unpredictable since I first started thinking about emergency preparedness. We now face not just traditional natural disasters like earthquakes and hurricanes, but cyber attacks that can shut down power grids, supply chain disruptions that empty store shelves, and extreme weather events that seem to happen with increasing frequency.

The concept of a "bug out bag" (also called a go-bag or evacuation bag) has evolved since the early 2000s. What used to be primarily a military or extreme prepper concept has become mainstream emergency preparedness wisdom. FEMA, the Red Cross, and local emergency management agencies now routinely recommend that every household maintain ready-to-go emergency kits.

A bug out bag is a portable survival kit containing everything you need to sustain yourself for 72 hours if you have to evacuate your home quickly. The "72 hours" isn't arbitrary (it's based on emergency management research showing that's how long it takes for organized relief efforts to reach disaster areas and begin providing assistance to displaced residents).

Modern bug out bags need to account for realities that didn't exist even a decade ago. We're more dependent on electronic devices for communication and navigation. Supply chains are more fragile, meaning stores may be empty for longer periods. Climate change has made weather more extreme and unpredictable. And unfortunately, we also have to consider human-caused emergencies like active shooter situations or terrorist attacks that might require rapid evacuation.

How to Use This Guide

This guide takes everything I've learned from both personal disaster experiences and professional emergency management training and updates it for 2026 realities. You'll notice I don't include long itemized lists like many survival guides. Instead, I'll walk you through the thinking process behind each category of supplies, explain the trade-offs you need to consider, and help you make decisions based on your specific situation, region, and family needs.

Every recommendation comes from either personal experience or professional research. When I suggest a type of water purification tablet, it's because I've tested them. When I recommend bag features, it's because I've carried heavy packs through difficult terrain. When I discuss food choices, it's based on what sustained me during multi-day emergencies.

The goal isn't to turn you into a survival expert overnight. It's to help you think through emergency scenarios systematically so you can prepare for your situation. Whether you live in earthquake country like I once did, hurricane territory along the coasts, tornado alley in the midwest, or anywhere else disasters might strike, this guide will help you build a bug out bag that could save your life.

We'll focus on practical preparedness that fits into normal life. You don't need to build an underground bunker or spend thousands of dollars. You need thoughtful preparation that gives you options when circumstances force you to leave home quickly. Because as I learned during that earthquake, when disaster strikes, you don't get to choose the timing or the circumstances. You only get to choose how ready you are.

Chapter 1: Choosing Your Bug Out Bag

Bag Selection Criteria

The bag itself is probably going to be the most expensive part of your bug out kit, so don't cheap out here. During a disaster, you don't want your bag falling apart when you need it most. I learned this lesson during my hiking days in the mountains around Lake Arrowhead.

I'd bought what I thought was a decent hiking pack from a discount sporting goods store for about thirty bucks. It looked sturdy enough in the store, had plenty of pockets, and seemed like a good deal. Three miles into a day hike in the San Bernardino Mountains, one of the shoulder straps tore completely off. I spent the rest of that hike carrying a heavy pack by the remaining strap and the top handle, turning what should have been an enjoyable eight-mile loop into a painful ordeal that left my back sore for days.

Don't buy your bug out bag at a discount store. A bug out bag isn't luggage you're dragging through an airport. You might need to carry it for miles on foot, possibly over rough terrain, while you're stressed, tired, and dealing with an emergency situation.

First, consider how you'll use the bag. If you're planning to drive during an evacuation, weight becomes less critical than storage capacity and organization. But if there's any chance you'll need to carry it on foot (power outages make elevators unusable, debris can block roads, or you might not have access to a vehicle), then weight and comfort become everything.

Your bag needs to be grab-and-go ready at all times. This means easily accessible in your home, not buried in a closet under Christmas decorations. I keep mine in the hall closet near the front door, where I can reach it even in the dark. Some people store theirs in the garage, but garage doors might not work during power outages, and you don't want to be hunting around for manual releases when you're trying to evacuate quickly.

The bag should be large enough to hold 72 hours' worth of supplies for each person it's intended to serve, but not so large that it becomes unwieldy. A good rule of thumb: a fully loaded bug out bag shouldn't weigh more than 20-25% of your body weight if you need to carry it. For most adults, this means keeping the total weight under 35-40 pounds.

Recommended Bag Types

I've tested dozens of different bag styles over the years, from military surplus rucksacks to high-end hiking backpacks to rolling duffel bags. Each has advantages and disadvantages depending on your situation.

Rolling duffel bags work well if you're planning to evacuate by vehicle. These bags offer the most storage space for the money, and the wheels make them easy to transport across smooth surfaces. I used one for several years when I lived in an apartment complex with long hallways and elevator access. The external pockets made it easy to access frequently rotated items like food and batteries without unpacking the entire bag.

The downside of wheeled bags becomes obvious the moment you hit stairs, curbs, or any kind of rough terrain. During the Northridge earthquake, many people found themselves having to abandon their wheeled luggage because debris made the streets impassable for anything with wheels. If you choose a wheeled bag, make sure it also has backpack straps as a backup option.

Traditional hiking backpacks offer the best option if there's any chance you'll need to travel on foot. A good backpack distributes weight properly across your hips and shoulders, making it possible to carry heavier loads comfortably for longer distances. The frame (either internal or external) provides structure and prevents the bag from becoming a shapeless blob that shifts around as you walk.

I use a 65-liter internal frame hiking pack that I picked up during an REI member sale. That's my preference, but surplus stores, thrift shops, and discount sporting goods chains all carry functional packs at a fraction of that price. The construction standards described later in this chapter apply regardless of where you buy. It's probably overkill for most bug out scenarios, but after carrying inadequate packs through the mountains for years, I'd take too much capacity over too little. The pack has a built-in rain cover, multiple access points (you can reach items in the middle without unpacking everything from the top), and compression straps that let me reduce the bulk when it's not fully loaded.

Military surplus stores offer another option worth considering. Surplus packs are built to withstand abuse and are often available at reasonable prices. The downside is they're designed for young soldiers in peak physical condition, not for civilians who might be dealing with age, injuries, or health conditions. Military packs also tend to be heavier than civilian alternatives and may lack some of the comfort features that make long carries bearable.

Some people swear by tactical-style packs, splitting the difference between military surplus and civilian hiking gear. These bags often have MOLLE webbing that allows you to attach pouches and gear externally. While this modularity can be useful, it also adds complexity and potential failure points. Unless you're already familiar with tactical gear systems, a traditional hiking pack is probably a better choice.

Size and Weight Considerations

Getting the size right requires balancing competing priorities. Too small, and you can't carry everything you need. Too large, and the bag becomes too heavy or unwieldy to manage effectively. The sweet spot for most people falls somewhere between 40 and 70 liters of capacity.

I learned about weight considerations during a weekend camping trip in Joshua Tree National Park. I'd loaded my pack with what seemed like reasonable supplies: three days of food, extra water, a sleeping bag, tent, and various other gear. By the time I'd hiked four miles into the desert, the pack felt like it had gained fifty pounds. Every step became a struggle, and what should have been an enjoyable hike turned into an endurance test.

That experience taught me to weigh everything that goes into a pack and to test the loaded weight before heading out. A bug out bag that sits in your closet for months at the perfect weight can become unbearable if you add "just one more thing" without removing something else.

The 72-hour supply guideline translates differently depending on your situation. A single person in good health can get by with a smaller, lighter kit than a family with children or elderly members. Someone with medical conditions requiring daily medications needs more space than someone who's generally healthy. People living in cold climates need more space for warm clothing than those in temperate areas.

Weight distribution matters as much as total weight. A 40-pound pack that's properly balanced and fitted can be more comfortable than a 30-pound pack that's poorly organized. Heavy items should be packed close to your back and centered between your shoulder blades. Sleeping bags and bulky items go at the bottom, frequently needed items stay accessible near the top or in external pockets.

When testing your packed bag, don't just lift it and decide it feels okay. Put it on properly (loosen all straps, put arms through shoulder straps, fasten hip belt, then tighten shoulder straps and load lifters), and walk around your neighborhood for at least 30 minutes. If it's uncomfortable during a casual neighborhood walk, it'll be unbearable during an emergency when you're stressed and possibly walking much longer distances.

Durability and Weather Resistance

Your bug out bag might sit unused for years before you need it, then suddenly face extreme conditions when disaster strikes. The bag needs to withstand long-term storage without degrading, then perform flawlessly when you finally need it.

I learned about durability during the forest fire that trapped me on the mountain road. After the helicopter water drop that saved my life, I realized everything in my car was soaked. If I'd been on foot with a bug out bag, those supplies would have needed to survive being drenched. A bag that leaks or falls apart when wet could turn a survivable situation into a deadly one.

Look for bags made from ripstop nylon or similar heavy-duty materials. The fabric should feel substantial without being unnecessarily heavy. Zippers are often the first thing to fail on bags, so examine them carefully. YKK zippers are generally reliable, and larger zipper teeth tend to be more durable than fine ones. Double-zipper pulls (where two zipper pulls meet in the middle) let you access the bag from either direction and provide redundancy if one pull breaks.

Water resistance comes in different levels. Truly waterproof bags are available but tend to be expensive and often sacrifice breathability (leading to condensation problems). Water-resistant fabric with good water-repellent coatings will handle most conditions you're likely to encounter. Many hiking packs include rain covers that pull over the entire bag during heavy weather, providing an extra layer of protection.

Seam construction matters more than most people realize. Stress points where straps attach to the bag body should be reinforced with extra stitching or fabric patches. I've seen bags fail at these connection points when they're loaded heavily or handled roughly. Look for bartack stitching (dense zigzag stitching) at stress points and avoid bags where straps appear to be simply sewn on with a straight line of stitches.

The frame system (if the bag has one) should be adjustable to fit different torso lengths. An ill-fitting pack will be uncomfortable no matter how well it's made. Many outdoor gear stores offer fitting services where staff can adjust the pack to your measurements. This service is worth using for packs you're planning to rely on in emergency situations.

Consider how the bag will age. Fabrics can degrade from UV exposure if the bag is stored in areas with direct sunlight. Rubber and plastic components (zippers, buckles, and waterproof coatings) can become brittle, especially in temperature extremes. Plan to inspect your bag at least twice a year and replace it if you notice signs of deterioration that could lead to failure when you need it most.

Chapter 2: Water and Hydration

Water Storage Solutions

Water is the most critical item in your bug out bag, but it's also the heaviest and most problematic to store long-term. I learned this during a hiking mishap in Joshua Tree when a flash flood threatened the canyon I was in and I had to move fast to higher ground. I'd brought what I thought was plenty of water for a day hike, but when conditions forced me out of the canyon quickly, every ounce in my pack suddenly mattered.

Here's the brutal math: water weighs about eight pounds per gallon. If you're planning for the standard 72-hour emergency kit and following the recommended one gallon per person per day, you're looking at 24 pounds of water alone. Add that to everything else you need to carry, and you're quickly approaching the weight limits of what most people can manage on foot.

This is why I don't recommend storing much water directly in your bug out bag. Instead, I keep four standard water bottles in my pack, giving me enough for about a day at most. The real water storage happens near the bag, not in it. I keep several one-gallon jugs in the same closet as my bug out bag, and the plan is to grab those jugs and throw them in the car trunk during an evacuation.

If you're evacuating by vehicle, water storage becomes much easier. A case of individual water bottles works well because they're already portioned out and easy to distribute among family members. Those five-gallon water cooler jugs that get delivered to offices are another good option if you have the space. They're stable, have handles for carrying, and provide a substantial amount of water in a single container.

For the water you do store in your bag, rotation is critical. Water doesn't exactly "expire," but it can become contaminated or develop an off taste if stored too long in plastic containers. I learned this during one of my CERT training exercises when we were given water that had been sitting in someone's emergency kit for over two years. It was technically safe to drink, but it tasted like plastic and made several people nauseous.

Check the dates on your water bottles every six months and replace them as needed. This is easier if you choose a rotation system where you use the water from your kit during normal life, then replace it with fresh bottles. Some people set reminders on their phones twice a year when daylight saving time changes to check and rotate their emergency supplies.

The containers matter as much as the water itself. Cheap plastic bottles can split or leak, especially if they've been sitting in temperature extremes. I've had water bottles stored in my garage split along the seams during a hot summer, creating a mess and leaving me without the water I thought I had. If you're storing water long-term, invest in better containers designed for emergency storage.

Collapsible water containers are worth considering for your bug out bag because they take up minimal space when empty but can hold substantial amounts when filled. I carry a couple of collapsible bottles that can each hold a liter when filled. During normal times they're compressed flat in my pack, but if I find a water source during an emergency, I can fill them up and extend my water supply.

Water Purification Methods

No matter how much water you store, you might need more during an extended emergency. This is where water purification becomes essential. I carry multiple purification methods in my kit because redundancy matters when your life depends on clean water.

Water purification tablets are the simplest and most compact option. I keep two bottles of them in my bug out bag, enough to purify about 100 liters of water. These tablets work by releasing chemicals (usually iodine or chlorine compounds) that kill bacteria, viruses, and other pathogens. The process is simple: drop a tablet in a liter of water, wait about an hour, and the water should be safe to drink.

The waiting time is important and something many people forget during emergencies. I learned this during a camping trip when we ran low on clean water and had to purify some from a questionable stream. We were all thirsty and impatient, and someone in our group started drinking the water after only fifteen minutes. He spent the next day sick with stomach problems that could have been avoided by simply waiting the full hour for the tablets to work.

Purification tablets have limitations. They only work on biological contamination like bacteria and viruses. If the water contains dangerous chemicals, heavy metals, or other non-biological contaminants, tablets won't help. They also don't improve the taste of bad water, and in some cases they can make it worse. Iodine tablets leave a medicinal taste that some people find difficult to stomach.

Portable water filters offer another purification option that addresses some of the limitations of tablets. Modern hiking filters can remove bacteria, parasites, and many other contaminants while improving taste and clarity. I carry a small pump-style filter that can process about a liter of water in a few minutes with minimal effort.

The advantage of filters is that they work immediately (no waiting time like with tablets) and generally produce better-tasting water. The downside is that filters are larger and heavier than tablets, and they can clog or break if the source water is dirty. Some filters also don't remove viruses, which are smaller than the pore size of most filter media.

Boiling remains the most reliable method for killing biological contaminants, but it requires fuel and time that you might not have during an emergency. If you do need to boil water, remember that a rolling boil for one minute is sufficient at sea level, but you need to boil for three minutes at elevations above 6,500 feet.

I learned about the elevation requirement during a camping trip in the Sierra Nevada mountains. We'd been boiling water from a stream for what we thought was adequate time, but we were at about 8,000 feet elevation and only boiling for a minute or so. Several people in our group got sick with what we later figured out was probably giardia, a parasitic infection that causes severe diarrhea and stomach cramps.

UV sterilization pens represent a newer technology worth considering. These devices use ultraviolet light to kill pathogens in water without adding chemicals or requiring filtration. The process is fast (usually less than two minutes per liter) and doesn't affect the taste of the water. The downside is that UV pens require batteries and can be damaged if dropped or exposed to extreme conditions.

Modern Water Treatment Technology

Water treatment technology has advanced since I first started building emergency kits in the 1990s. Some of the newer options are worth considering, especially if you're building a complete long-term emergency kit.

Gravity-fed filtration systems have become popular among serious hikers and emergency preparedness enthusiasts. These systems use large capacity bags that you fill with source water, then hang above a clean collection container. Gravity pulls the water through the filter elements, producing clean water without manual pumping. The advantage is that you can process large quantities of water with minimal effort. The downside is bulk and weight, making them less suitable for bug out bags but excellent for base camp situations.

Water purification drops and liquids offer an alternative to tablets with some advantages. Liquid purifiers often work faster than tablets and may be more effective against certain types of contamination. They also don't have the shelf life limitations that tablets sometimes face. I keep a small bottle of water purification drops as a backup to my tablets.

Combination filter and purification systems address the limitations of using either filtration or chemical treatment alone. These systems use a filter to remove larger contaminants and improve taste, followed by UV sterilization or chemical treatment to kill pathogens that might pass through the filter.

While more complex and expensive than single-method systems, they provide the most complete water treatment available in portable formats.

Solar water disinfection is a low-tech method worth knowing about even though it's not practical for bug out bags. The process involves filling clear plastic bottles with water and exposing them to direct sunlight for several hours. The UV radiation and heat work together to kill pathogens. This method requires no supplies beyond clear bottles and sunlight, making it useful in situations where you have time but limited resources.

Reverse osmosis systems designed for emergency use have become smaller and more affordable in recent years. These systems can remove virtually all contaminants, including chemicals and heavy metals that other methods can't address. The trade-off is complexity, weight, and the need for water pressure to operate effectively.

Hydration Planning

Planning your water needs goes beyond just carrying enough for 72 hours. You need to think about how much water different activities require, how environmental conditions affect your needs, and how to recognize and prevent dehydration during stressful situations.

The standard recommendation of one gallon per person per day assumes normal activity levels and moderate climate conditions. If you're doing physical work, walking long distances with a heavy pack, or dealing with extreme heat, your water needs can easily double or triple. During my hiking days in the desert, I learned that I could go through a gallon of water in just a few hours of moderate hiking when temperatures were above 90 degrees.

Dehydration during emergencies is dangerous because it impairs judgment and physical performance when you need both most. I've seen people make increasingly poor decisions as they became more dehydrated during emergency response training exercises. What started as minor navigation errors progressed to dangerous choices that could have been fatal in a real emergency situation.

Early signs of dehydration include thirst (obviously), dark yellow urine, fatigue, and mild headaches. By the time you're experiencing these symptoms, you're already behind on fluid replacement. In emergency situations, it's better to drink water proactively instead of waiting until you feel thirsty.

Climate considerations dramatically affect hydration planning. Hot climates obviously increase water needs, but cold climates present their own challenges. You might not feel as thirsty in cold weather, but you're still losing water through respiration and sweating under winter clothing. High altitude also increases water needs because the dry air and increased breathing rate cause additional water loss.

Water discipline becomes important when you have limited supplies. This means rationing water appropriately while avoiding the mistake of under-hydrating to conserve supplies. Severe dehydration will incapacitate you faster than running out of water gradually while maintaining function.

During extended emergencies, finding additional water sources becomes critical. Natural sources like streams, lakes, and even rainwater can supplement your stored supplies, but they all require treatment before consumption. Urban sources might include water heaters, toilet tank reservoirs (not the bowl), and even swimming pools, though pool water requires extensive treatment and is not ideal for drinking.

Learning to identify potentially safe water sources is a skill worth developing before you need it. Fast-moving streams are generally safer than stagnant pools. Water from higher elevations is cleaner than water that has flowed through populated areas. Springs emerging directly from rock faces are often among the safest natural sources.

A hydration plan for your situation should account for your family members' individual needs, your local climate, likely evacuation routes, and potential water sources in your area.

Someone with medical conditions might need more water for medications. Elderly family members or young children might need different hydration approaches. People taking certain medications might have altered hydration needs.

Take your bug out bag on day hikes or camping trips and see how your water supplies hold up under real conditions. Problems with purification methods are better found during a Saturday hike than during an actual evacuation.

Chapter 3: Food and Nutrition

Emergency Food Selection

Food planning for a bug out bag is all about balancing calories, weight, shelf life, and taste. I learned this balance during that Christmas hike in 1986 when my father and I got trapped in the San Bernardino Mountains. We'd brought nothing but a few granola bars for what we thought would be a quick morning hike. By the time I was climbing out of that canyon in the snow to get help, I was running on empty and making decisions with a brain that wasn't getting enough fuel.

The first rule of emergency food is calories per ounce. When you're carrying everything on your back, every ounce counts. You want foods that pack the most energy into the smallest space and lightest weight. Fat contains more than twice as many calories per gram as carbohydrates or protein, which is why nuts, nut butters, and energy bars with high fat content are staples in most bug out bags.

I keep a variety of energy bars in my kit, but I've learned to be picky about which ones. During a weekend camping trip in the Mojave Desert, I discovered that some energy bars turn into inedible rocks when exposed to heat, while others become gooey messes. After that experience, I started testing different brands by leaving samples in my car during summer heat waves to see how they held up. The winners were bars that maintained their texture and taste even after sitting in 120-degree temperatures for hours.

Nuts and trail mix provide excellent calorie density and have impressive shelf lives when stored properly. I rotate through different types to avoid flavor fatigue, mixing almonds, cashews, dried fruit, and sometimes even some chocolate chips for morale. The key is buying nuts that are already roasted and salted, because raw nuts can go rancid more quickly and don't provide the sodium your body needs during stressful situations.

Jerky and other dried meats offer protein and satisfaction that plant-based foods can't match. During my CERT training, we did a 24-hour exercise where we could only eat what we'd brought in our emergency kits. The people who'd focused entirely on energy bars and crackers were dragging by hour 16, while those who'd included some protein sources maintained their energy levels much better.

Instant foods that only require hot water can expand your meal options without adding much weight. Instant oatmeal, dehydrated soups, and freeze-dried camping meals all work well if you have a way to heat water. The trade-off is that you now need to carry fuel and cooking equipment, adding weight and complexity to your kit.

Comfort foods deserve consideration even in emergency situations. I learned this during the Northridge earthquake when we were living without power for several days. The stress of the situation made everyone crave familiar, comforting foods. A few pieces of hard candy or some cookies might seem frivolous in an emergency kit, but they can provide a huge psychological boost when everything else in your world has gone wrong.

Consider how much preparation your chosen foods require. Anything that needs extensive cooking, mixing, or cleanup might not be practical during an emergency evacuation. You want foods you can eat directly from the package with minimal fuss. This is especially important if you're eating while walking or if you don't have access to clean water for food preparation.

Modern MREs and Alternatives

Military MREs (Meals Ready to Eat) have come a long way since the early versions that soldiers joked were "Meals Rejected by Everyone." Modern MREs provide complete, balanced meals that can be eaten cold or heated with the included chemical heating packs. I've tested dozens of different MRE varieties over the years, and while they're not going to win any culinary awards, they're better than their reputation suggests.

The main advantage of MREs is convenience and completeness. Each meal provides roughly 1,200-1,300 calories along with an entrée, side dish, crackers, spread, dessert, and accessories like spoons and napkins. The chemical heaters work reliably and can warm a meal to a comfortable eating temperature in about 10-15 minutes without requiring any external fuel source.

I keep three MREs in my bug out bag, providing one full day of complete meals for one person. The downside is weight and bulk. Three MREs weigh about four pounds and take up space in a pack. They're also more expensive per calorie than most other emergency food options.

Civilian MRE alternatives have proliferated in recent years, offering similar convenience with often better taste. Companies like Mountain House, Backpacker's Pantry, and others produce freeze-dried meals designed for hikers and campers. These meals are lighter than military MREs and offer more variety in flavors and dietary options.

Freeze-dried camping meals require hot water for preparation, which means you need a stove and fuel. But they're lighter than traditional MREs and often taste better. I learned to appreciate these during my extensive hiking days in the Sierra Nevada. After carrying heavy packs for miles, the weight savings of freeze-dried meals became very apparent.

Some of the newer emergency food products are designed for long-term storage instead of immediate consumption. These products often come in large containers or pouches designed to feed families for weeks or months. While not practical for bug out bags due to size and weight, they're worth considering for home emergency supplies that could supplement your mobile kit.

Homemade alternatives can work well if you have the time and inclination to prepare them. During my disaster recovery planning days at Trader Joe's, I experimented with making my own emergency food packages using vacuum sealers and shelf-stable ingredients. Combinations like peanut butter and crackers, dried fruit and nuts, or even pasta and shelf-stable sauce can provide variety and familiarity at lower cost than commercial options.

The key with any prepared meal option is testing them before you need them. I make it a point to eat one MRE or freeze-dried meal every few months, both to check that they're still good and to remind myself what they taste like. There's nothing worse than being hungry and stressed during an emergency and discovering that your emergency food is inedible or has gone bad.

Nutritional Considerations

Emergency nutrition goes beyond just getting enough calories. During stressful situations, your body has different nutritional needs, and the foods you choose can affect your energy levels, decision-making ability, and overall health during critical times.

Protein becomes especially important during emergencies because stress increases your body's protein requirements. When I was stranded in that canyon with my father, I could feel my strength and mental clarity declining as the hours passed without adequate nutrition. Protein helps maintain muscle function and provides sustained energy that pure carbohydrates can't match.

Sodium needs increase during emergencies, especially if you're sweating more than usual or dealing with physical stress. This is one area where processed emergency foods have an advantage over fresh alternatives. Most MREs and energy bars contain substantial amounts of sodium, which your body needs to maintain proper fluid balance and nerve function.

Blood sugar stability affects your decision-making ability, which can be critical during emergencies. Foods that cause rapid spikes and crashes in blood sugar can leave you feeling weak and unable to think clearly when you need your wits most. Complex carbohydrates and foods that combine carbs with protein or fat provide more stable energy levels.

I learned about blood sugar effects during a long day of emergency response training. We'd been given energy drinks and candy bars for lunch, and by mid-afternoon, half the training group was experiencing what felt like hypoglycemic crashes. People were making basic errors in judgment and having trouble concentrating on simple tasks. The instructors had planned this deliberately to demonstrate how poor nutrition affects performance under stress.

Fiber seems unimportant until your gut disagrees with three days of unfamiliar emergency food. Many emergency foods are low in fiber, which creates digestive problems at exactly the wrong moment. This matters more if your kit relies heavily on MREs or processed bars rather than foods close to your normal diet.

Vitamins and minerals matter more during stress than during normal times. B vitamins are depleted during stressful situations, and deficiencies can affect energy levels and mental function. While a 72-hour emergency probably won't cause serious vitamin deficiencies, choosing foods that provide some nutritional variety can help maintain your health and energy.

Caffeine considerations deserve attention if you're a regular coffee or soda drinker. Caffeine withdrawal can cause headaches, fatigue, and irritability, which are the last things you need during an emergency. I keep instant coffee packets in my emergency kit not because I love instant coffee, but because I know I'll function better with some caffeine than without it if I'm already dealing with emergency stress.

Special dietary needs become more challenging during emergencies but can't be ignored. People with diabetes need to carefully plan their emergency food to manage blood sugar levels. Those with food allergies need to read labels carefully and possibly carry additional medications. Vegetarians and vegans need to ensure they have adequate protein sources that don't require refrigeration.

Food Storage and Rotation

Food storage for emergency kits requires different thinking than normal pantry management. You're optimizing for shelf life, temperature stability, and space efficiency instead of convenience and variety. I learned this during my early emergency preparedness days when I discovered that half the food in my first emergency kit had gone bad because I hadn't thought through storage conditions properly.

Temperature fluctuations are the enemy of long-term food storage. My garage, where I initially stored emergency supplies, regularly swung from freezing in winter to over 100 degrees in summer. This temperature cycling accelerated the degradation of everything from energy bars to canned goods. Foods that should have lasted years were going bad in months.

Rodent protection is essential if you're storing food anywhere that mice or rats might have access. I learned this lesson when I discovered that mice had chewed through supposedly sealed packages and contaminated an entire emergency food cache. Now all my stored food goes into hard plastic containers or metal cans that rodents can't penetrate.

Rotation schedules prevent waste and ensure your emergency food is always fresh. I use the "first in, first out" principle that I learned during my years in the computer industry managing data backups. Every six months, I eat the oldest items from my emergency kit and replace them with fresh supplies. This system ensures I never have food sitting around for years getting stale.

Dating everything is important for effective rotation. I use a permanent marker to write purchase dates on all packages, even if they already have expiration dates printed on them. This makes it easy to identify the oldest items during rotation checks. Some people use colored dots or tape to indicate different purchase dates, which can work well if you buy emergency supplies in batches.

Packaging integrity affects shelf life as much as the food itself. Even if food is technically still good, damaged packaging can lead to contamination or accelerated spoilage. I inspect all packages during rotation checks and replace anything with tears, dents, or other damage that could compromise the contents.

Storage location affects both accessibility and preservation. Your emergency food needs to be easily accessible during an emergency, but it also needs to be protected from temperature extremes and pests. I keep my bug out bag food in the same climate-controlled area where I store the bag itself, while larger emergency food supplies go in a cool, dry area of my house.

Consider seasonal adjustments to your food rotation. Foods that work well in winter might not hold up during summer heat waves, and vice versa. I learned this when energy bars I'd stored during cool weather turned into inedible mush during the first hot day of summer. Now I rotate certain items seasonally instead of just based on expiration dates.

I eat samples from my emergency supply every few months, both to check quality and to remind myself how these foods actually taste. An energy bar that turns to chalk after six months in the garage is something you want to find out about during a routine check, not when you're hungry and stressed and there's nothing else to eat.

Chapter 4: Power, Light, and Communication

Modern Lighting Solutions

When Hurricane Milton hit my Florida apartment, the first thing I noticed after the wind and rain died down wasn't the damage or the mess. It was how completely dark everything was. The power had gone out instantly, and without any streetlights or house lights, it was darker than I'd ever experienced in an urban area. I stumbled around my apartment, trying to assess the damage while carefully navigating the debris the storm had shifted across the floor.

Reliable lighting isn't just convenient during an emergency, it's essential for safety. You can't navigate hazards you can't see, and you can't assess your situation or make good decisions when you're stumbling around in the dark.

LED technology has revolutionized emergency lighting since my early preparedness days. The first flashlight I bought for emergency use in the 1990s used incandescent bulbs and ate through batteries faster than I could replace them. Modern LED lights provide brighter illumination while using a fraction of the power, meaning your batteries last much longer when you need them most.

I keep multiple lighting sources in my bug out bag because redundancy matters when you can't just flip a switch. My primary light is a high-quality LED headlamp that leaves both hands free for other tasks. During that mountain rescue when I had to climb out of the canyon to get help for my father, I was constantly needing my hands for balance and climbing while also needing to see where I was going. A handheld flashlight would have been nearly useless in that situation.

The headlamp I use now has multiple brightness settings and a red light mode that preserves night vision. I learned about the importance of red light during my CERT training when we practiced search and rescue operations in darkened buildings.

White light destroys your night vision for several minutes after you turn it off, leaving you blind if you need to move around without the light. Red light allows you to see what you're doing without ruining your natural night vision.

Backup lighting is just as important as your primary light. I carry a smaller backup LED flashlight and a couple of those little keychain lights that seem almost too small to be useful. Even a tiny light is invaluable when your main light fails or when you need to mark your location for rescuers.

Battery compatibility across your lighting equipment saves weight and simplifies your power management. All my lights use either AA or AAA batteries, so I don't need to carry multiple types of spare batteries. Some people prefer lights that use CR123 lithium batteries because they have longer shelf life and better performance in cold weather, but those batteries are more expensive and harder to find than standard alkalines.

Solar-powered lights have become much more practical in recent years. I have a small solar lantern that charges during the day and provides ambient lighting at night. It's not bright enough for navigation or detailed work, but it's perfect for general camp lighting and it doesn't consume any of my finite battery supply. The solar panel is built right into the lantern, so there are no separate components to lose or break.

Your lighting needs break into three modes: a bright focused beam for navigation and spotting things at distance, diffused area light for camp tasks and general use, and low-level light for map reading or detailed work that preserves your night vision. Most modern emergency lights cover all three.

Portable Power Systems

The modern world runs on electricity, and emergencies don't change that fact. During the days after the Northridge earthquake, one of the most frustrating aspects was having electronic devices that could have been useful if only they had power. My portable radio died after a few hours, my camera ran out of battery just when I needed to document damage for insurance purposes, and we had no way to charge anything.

Portable power systems have evolved dramatically since then. What used to require car-sized batteries and inverters can now be accomplished with devices small enough to fit in your pocket. Power banks have shrunk dramatically while their capacity has grown. The ones available now would have seemed like science fiction compared to what existed when I was dealing with the Northridge aftermath.

I carry two different power banks in my bug out bag. A small one about the size of a deck of cards that can charge my phone twice, and a larger one that's about the size of a paperback book but can charge multiple devices several times. The smaller one stays easily accessible in an outside pocket for quick phone charging, while the larger one serves as my main power reserve.

Battery capacity is measured in milliamp hours (mAh), and the number matters when you're choosing a power bank. A typical smartphone battery is around 3,000-4,000 mAh, so a 10,000 mAh power bank should theoretically charge your phone about 2-3 times. In reality, you lose some capacity to heat and conversion inefficiency, so figure on about 60-70% of the rated capacity being useful.

Power bank quality varies enormously, and cheap ones can be dangerous. I learned this when a bargain power bank I'd bought online started getting uncomfortably hot while charging and eventually stopped working entirely. Reputable brands cost more but use better battery cells and safety circuits that prevent overheating, overcharging, and other problems that can damage your devices or even cause fires.

USB charging has become the standard for most small electronic devices, simplifying your power planning. Everything from phones to GPS units to emergency radios can be charged from a USB power bank. This means you can carry one power source instead of multiple device-specific chargers.

Hand-crank generators offer a backup power option that doesn't depend on stored energy. These devices let you generate power by turning a crank, producing enough electricity to charge a phone or power a radio for short periods. The downside is that it takes a lot of cranking to generate meaningful amounts of power. I tested one during a camping trip and found that it took about 10 minutes of steady cranking to generate enough power for a 5-minute phone call.

If you have vehicle access during an emergency, your car's electrical system can run for hours without the engine. Most cars will power a USB charger long enough to top off a phone or two without risking the starting battery. I keep a car charger in my vehicle kit as a backup to the power banks in my bug out bag.

Solar Charging Options

Solar charging technology has reached the point where it's practical for emergency use, though it's not the cure-all that some people imagine. I first experimented with solar chargers during my extensive hiking days in the Sierra Nevada, where I was often away from power sources for days at a time.

Modern solar panels designed for portable use are much more efficient than the early versions I tried in the 1990s. Those early panels were heavy, fragile, and produced minimal power unless conditions were perfect. Current panels can charge devices even in partially cloudy conditions and are built to withstand outdoor use.

The solar charger I carry now is about the size of a tablet when folded and has four panels that unfold to about the size of a laptop. It can charge my phone directly from sunlight in about the same time as a wall charger, assuming good sun conditions. In cloudy weather or partial shade, charging takes much longer, but it still works.

Solar charging works best when combined with a power bank instead of charging devices directly. Solar output varies constantly based on sun angle, clouds, and shadows, confusing some devices or causing charging to stop and start repeatedly. It's better to use solar to charge a power bank during the day, then use the power bank to charge your devices when needed.

Panel positioning matters more than most people realize. Even partial shading of a solar panel can dramatically reduce output. During one camping trip, I couldn't figure out why my solar panel wasn't charging properly until I realized that a small tree branch was casting a shadow on just one corner of the panel. Moving the panel a few feet to avoid the shadow doubled the charging rate.

Weather considerations limit solar charging effectiveness. Obviously, solar panels don't work at night, but they also work poorly in heavy overcast conditions or during storms when you might need power most. This is why solar should supplement, not replace, other power sources in your emergency kit.

Maintenance and durability are important factors for solar equipment. Dust, dirt, and scratches on the panel surface reduce efficiency. Some panels come with cleaning cloths or have surfaces that shed dirt easily. The electrical connections are often the weakest point, so look for panels with sturdy connectors and consider carrying spare cables.

Emergency Communication Devices

Communication during emergencies serves multiple purposes. You need to receive information about the emergency situation, evacuation orders, or safety instructions. You need to communicate with family members who might be separated from you. And you might need to call for help if you're injured or stranded.

Cell phones are most people's primary communication device, but cell networks often fail during major emergencies. During the Northridge earthquake, the cell towers that were still standing were completely overloaded, making phone calls nearly impossible for the first several hours. Text messages sometimes got through when voice calls couldn't, because they use less network capacity.

I learned during the forest fire incident that trapped me on the mountain that even when cell networks are working, you might not have coverage in remote areas. That firefighter who jumped in my car and directed me to safety had a radio that could reach the incident command post, but my cell phone showed no signal at all.

Starlink and other satellite internet services have changed the emergency communication landscape in recent years. Unlike traditional cell networks that depend on ground-based towers, satellite internet can work anywhere with a clear view of the sky. I've seen Starlink terminals providing internet access in disaster zones where all other communication infrastructure was destroyed. The downside is cost and power consumption. The terminals aren't cheap, and they draw power that might be hard to maintain during extended emergencies.

Battery-powered AM/FM radios remain one of the most reliable ways to receive emergency information. Radio stations often stay on the air during disasters using backup power, and radio signals can reach areas where cell towers have failed. I keep a small digital radio in my bug out bag that can run for days on a couple of AA batteries.

Weather radios designed for emergency use can receive NOAA weather broadcasts and emergency alerts. These radios can wake themselves up when emergency alerts are broadcast, ensuring you get critical information even if you're not actively listening. Some models can also charge phones via USB, combining multiple functions in one device.

Two-way radios (walkie-talkies) allow communication between family members when cell networks are down. During my CERT training, we used FRS (Family Radio Service) radios to coordinate our response teams. These radios have limited range (1-3 miles depending on terrain), but they work independently of any infrastructure.

Amateur radio represents the most capable emergency communication option, but it requires a license and knowledge to use effectively. Ham radio operators often provide emergency communication services during disasters when other systems fail. While getting a ham radio license might be overkill for most people, it's worth knowing that this resource exists in many communities.

Satellite communication devices have become more affordable and practical for civilian emergency use. Personal satellite messengers can send preset emergency messages or GPS coordinates to rescue services even when you have no cell coverage. The more advanced models allow two-way text messaging with family members. The downside is ongoing subscription costs for the satellite service.

Navigation Tools

GPS has made navigation seem effortless, but GPS systems can fail during emergencies. Satellites might be disrupted, your device might break or run out of power, or atmospheric conditions might interfere with signal reception. I learned this during a hiking trip in the Sierra Nevada when my GPS unit died due to cold weather, leaving me without any electronic navigation aids.

Backup navigation methods become critical when electronic systems fail. I always carry a detailed paper map of my local area and any regions I might travel through during an evacuation. These maps don't require power, can't be hacked or jammed, and provide a much broader view of the terrain than a small GPS screen.

Compass navigation is a skill worth learning even in the GPS age. A simple orienteering compass weighs almost nothing and will work reliably for decades without maintenance. During my CERT training, we practiced navigation exercises where we had to find locations using only a map and compass. It's harder than it looks if you're not used to it.

Road atlases provide broader geographic context than local maps and can help you plan alternate routes if main highways are blocked. During major evacuations, the primary evacuation routes often become gridlocked or impassable. Having a good road atlas lets you identify back roads and alternate routes that might be less congested.

Offline GPS apps on your phone provide a compromise between electronic convenience and independence from data networks. These apps download map data to your phone's memory, so they work even when you have no cell signal. I use an app that lets me download detailed maps of my entire region, turning my phone into a capable GPS unit that works anywhere.

GPS coordinates become important if you need to communicate your location to emergency responders. In remote areas or during chaotic emergency situations, street addresses might not be useful. Knowing how to find and communicate your GPS coordinates can be the difference between being found quickly or waiting hours for help.

Learning to read terrain features helps with navigation when you don't have detailed maps. Understanding how contour lines show elevation, how valleys and ridges relate to water flow, and how human infrastructure follows terrain patterns can help you navigate even with crude maps or sketches.

Landmark identification and route marking techniques can help you navigate in unfamiliar areas or help others follow your route. During that mountain rescue when I had to climb out of the canyon to get help, I marked my route with rocks and broken branches so the rescue team could follow the same path to reach my father.

Practice navigation skills before you need them in an emergency. Try finding your way around your neighborhood using only a map and compass, or practice using your backup navigation tools during camping trips or day hikes. Like any skill, navigation becomes much more difficult under stress if you haven't practiced it beforehand.

Chapter 5: Shelter and Weather Protection

Emergency Shelter Options

Shelter becomes critical when you can't get back to your home or when your home is no longer safe. I learned this during the forest fire that trapped me on the mountain road between Lake Arrowhead and San Bernardino. Even though I was rescued relatively quickly, I realized afterward how exposed I would have been if I'd had to spend the night outdoors with no protection from the elements.

The key to emergency shelter is understanding that you're not trying to recreate the comfort of home. You're trying to create a microenvironment that protects you from wind, rain, cold, and heat long enough to either get rescued or reach safety. This is about survival, not camping comfort.

Space blankets (also called emergency blankets or mylar blankets) are probably the most compact shelter option you can carry. These thin sheets of reflective material fold down to the size of a deck of cards but can provide protection from wind and help retain body heat. I learned about their effectiveness during a CERT training exercise where we had to spend several hours outdoors in cold, windy conditions. The people with space blankets stayed much warmer than those without them.

The downside of space blankets is that they're fragile and noisy. They tear easily if you're not careful, and they crackle loudly in the wind, creating psychological irritation when you're already stressed. Despite these limitations, their weight-to-protection ratio is unmatched, so I keep several in my bug out bag.

Emergency bivvy sacks offer a step up in protection and durability. These are sleeping bag-shaped bags made from waterproof, breathable materials. You climb inside one and it creates a protective cocoon around your entire body. I tested one during a camping trip in the Sierra Nevada when unexpected weather moved in. The bivvy kept me dry and warm through a night of rain and wind that would have been miserable with just a space blanket.

Lightweight tarps provide versatility that other emergency shelters don't match. A good tarp can be configured as a lean-to, an A-frame shelter, or even a basic tent depending on what you need and what materials you have available for support. During my hiking days, I carried a small silnylon tarp that weighed less than a pound but could be set up in dozens of different configurations.

The challenge with tarps is that they require practice. You need to know a few basic knots and be able to identify anchor points for guy lines. Set up your tarp in the backyard during different weather until you can do it fast and without thinking about it. That's the threshold that matters.

Emergency tube tents offer a compromise between simplicity and protection. These are plastic tubes that you crawl inside, with one end closed and the other end that you can seal behind you. They're lightweight, completely waterproof, and require no setup skills. The downside is that they're claustrophobic and provide minimal insulation beyond blocking wind and rain.

Pre-made emergency shelters designed for survival situations have become more sophisticated in recent years. Some are inflatable and can be set up quickly without tools or guy lines. Others use lightweight poles and clips similar to backpacking tents but in much more compact packages. These shelters cost more than basic options like space blankets, but they offer better protection and are easier to use under stress.

Weather-Specific Gear

Different weather conditions require different approaches to protection, and what works in one situation might be dangerous in another. I learned this lesson during various outdoor experiences in different climates and seasons around Southern California and the Southwest.

Rain gear becomes essential when you're dealing with wet conditions, but not all rain gear is created equal. During one of my hiking trips in the mountains, I got caught in an unexpected downpour while wearing a cheap plastic rain poncho. The poncho kept the rain off initially, but within an hour I was soaked from my own sweat because the plastic didn't breathe at all. I ended up wetter inside the poncho than I would have been in the rain.

Modern rain gear uses breathable waterproof fabrics that allow moisture vapor to escape while keeping liquid water out. These materials cost more than simple plastic, but they're much more comfortable during extended use. I now carry a lightweight rain jacket made from one of these breathable fabrics, and it's made a huge difference in comfort during wet weather.

Wind protection often gets overlooked, but wind can kill you faster than rain in many situations. Wind strips away your body heat through convection and can make even moderate temperatures dangerous. During that Christmas hike when my father and I got trapped in the canyon, the wind was probably more dangerous than the cold temperature itself.

A simple windbreaker can make an enormous difference in comfort and safety. The material doesn't need to be waterproof or expensive, it just needs to block wind from reaching your body. Some emergency shelters are designed primarily for wind protection instead of rain protection, recognizing that wind is often the more immediate threat.

Cold weather gear runs on a three-layer system: a base layer that pulls moisture off your skin, an insulating layer that traps warm air, and an outer layer that blocks wind and rain. The logic is that you can peel off or add layers as your exertion level and the temperature shift, which a single heavy parka can't do.

I learned about layering during winter camping trips in the mountains. The temperature can swing 40 degrees between day and night, and your activity level affects how much heat you're generating. A system that keeps you warm while you're sleeping might cause dangerous overheating when you're hiking with a heavy pack.

Hot weather protection focuses on different priorities: blocking solar radiation, allowing air circulation, and managing sweat. Light-colored, loose-fitting clothing that covers your skin provides better protection than shorts and t-shirts, even though it seems counterintuitive. During my desert hiking days, I learned that exposed skin loses water faster and is more vulnerable to heat-related problems.

Shade creation becomes critical in hot climates when natural shade isn't available. A lightweight tarp or emergency shelter can be rigged to create shade during the hottest parts of the day. This isn't just about comfort; in extreme heat, shade can be the difference between maintaining your ability to function and succumbing to heat exhaustion.

Thermal Regulation

Your body's ability to maintain proper temperature is what keeps you alive, and emergency situations can quickly push you outside your thermal comfort zone. Understanding how your body gains and loses heat helps you make better decisions about shelter and clothing during emergencies.

Heat loss happens through four main mechanisms: conduction (direct contact with cold objects), convection (air movement), radiation (heat radiating away from your body), and evaporation (sweating and breathing). Each of these can be managed with proper gear and techniques.

Conduction becomes a major problem when you're in contact with cold ground or other surfaces. During that night in the canyon when my father had his apparent heart attack, he was lying directly on the cold ground and losing tremendous amounts of body heat through conduction. The pile of leaves that covered him provided some insulation from the ground, probably helping save his life.

Ground insulation is often more important than top insulation in emergency situations. A simple foam pad or even a thick layer of pine needles can dramatically reduce heat loss to the ground. I carry a lightweight closed-cell foam pad in my bug out bag that weighs almost nothing but provides important insulation when I need to sit or lie on cold surfaces.

Convection control is what most people think of as "staying out of the wind," but it also includes managing air movement inside your clothing and shelter. Dead air space is what insulates you, so anything that prevents air movement helps retain heat. This is why loose, fluffy insulation works better than compressed insulation, and why multiple thin layers often work better than one thick layer.

Your head radiates heat faster than most people expect because it has a dense network of blood vessels near the surface and usually wears no insulation. The old saying about losing most of your heat through your head is an exaggeration, but not by much. A knit cap is the cheapest warmth improvement you can make.

Emergency heat sources can be lifesavers in cold conditions, but they need to be used safely. Chemical hand warmers provide heat for several hours and are completely safe when used properly. I keep several in my bug out bag because they're lightweight and can provide important warmth to core areas or extremities when hypothermia becomes a concern.

Body heat sharing is an emergency technique that can be effective but requires some caution. Sharing a sleeping bag or shelter with another person can help both people stay warm, but it only works if at least one person is still generating adequate body heat. If both people are already hypothermic, sharing body heat won't help much.

Light exercise like isometric muscle contractions generates heat without producing sweat. That matters because sweat evaporating off your body pulls heat with it, which means vigorous exercise that soaks your base layer can leave you colder after you stop than before you started. Shiver actively if you're cold and stationary. Move just enough if you're mobile.

Sleep Systems

Sleep becomes both more important and more difficult during emergency situations. Your body needs rest to maintain its ability to make good decisions and regulate temperature, but stress and uncomfortable conditions can make sleep elusive. Having a plan for getting adequate rest can make the difference between maintaining your capabilities and deteriorating into poor judgment and hypothermia.

Sleep surfaces matter more than most people realize until they try sleeping on hard ground. During my early camping days, I thought I could tough it out sleeping directly on the ground, but I discovered that even one night without proper padding leaves you sore and tired the next day. In an emergency situation where you might need to walk long distances or perform physical tasks, starting the day already exhausted puts you at a serious disadvantage.

The sleeping pad I carry in my bug out bag is a closed-cell foam pad that's about three-quarters of an inch thick. It's not as comfortable as an air mattress, but it's completely reliable, provides good insulation from the ground, and can't be punctured or deflated. I learned to value reliability over comfort after an air mattress failure during a camping trip left me sleeping on bare ground in freezing temperatures.

Emergency sleeping bags come in different styles designed for different situations. Traditional sleeping bags provide the best warmth and comfort but take up space in a pack. Sleeping bag liners weigh much less and take up minimal space but provide limited warmth on their own. Emergency sleeping bags made from space blanket material are extremely compact but can be uncomfortable and noisy.

I carry a combination approach: a lightweight sleeping bag liner that can be used alone in mild conditions or combined with emergency shelters and space blankets for additional warmth when needed. This system is more versatile than a single heavy sleeping bag and allows me to adjust my sleep system based on conditions.

Temperature ratings on sleeping bags can be misleading because they're based on survival temperature, not comfort temperature. A sleeping bag rated to 20 degrees might keep you alive at 20 degrees, but you'll be cold and miserable. Most people need a sleeping bag rated 10-15 degrees colder than the temperature they expect to encounter for comfortable sleep.

Sleeping in emergencies requires different considerations than recreational camping. You might need to sleep in your clothes to be ready for quick movement. You might need to keep essential gear inside your sleeping system to prevent it from freezing or being lost. You might need to sleep in shifts if you're with other people to maintain security or watch for changing conditions.

Sleep position affects both warmth and safety in emergency situations. Sleeping curled up in a fetal position conserves body heat better than sleeping stretched out. Sleeping with your head slightly downhill prevents blood from pooling in your head and helps you sleep more comfortably. Sleeping with your back to the wind or weather reduces heat loss and discomfort.

Stress and unfamiliar surroundings make sleep harder even when you're physically wrecked. A familiar object from home helps more than it sounds like it should. During the days after the earthquake when we were sleeping in our car, I kept a small item from our apartment that I could hold, and it made the difference between lying awake for hours and actually falling asleep. A bedtime routine, even a minimal one, gives your brain the signal that sleep is the next thing.

Keeping your feet clean and dry matters more during emergencies than most people expect. Blisters and skin infections start fast when feet stay wet. Change socks before sleep even if you can't wash them. Dry is more important than clean in this context. A quick brush with a tiny bit of water keeps your mouth from developing problems that become genuinely distracting after a few days.

Chapter 6: Health and Hygiene

First Aid Essentials

Medical emergencies don't wait for convenient times, and during disasters, professional medical help might be hours or days away. I learned this lesson during the Northridge earthquake when my wife cut her feet on broken glass and we didn't even have a basic first aid kit in our apartment. I ended up using kitchen towels and Scotch tape to bandage her wounds, both ineffective and probably unsanitary.

First aid supplies aren't just nice to have during emergencies, they're essential. A relatively minor injury can become life-threatening if you can't control bleeding, prevent infection, or manage pain. During stressful emergency situations, people are more prone to accidents and injuries from moving quickly through unfamiliar or damaged environments.

The first aid kit I carry now is built around the most likely injuries I might encounter during an emergency evacuation. Cuts and scrapes from broken glass, debris, or falls. Burns from fires or hot surfaces. Sprains and strains from carrying heavy loads or walking on uneven terrain. Dehydration and heat exhaustion from physical exertion under stress. These aren't exotic wilderness medicine scenarios, they're common injuries that happen when normal life gets disrupted.

Wound care forms the foundation of any practical first aid kit. I learned about wound management during my CERT training, where we practiced treating simulated injuries with limited supplies. The basic principles are simple: stop bleeding, clean the wound, prevent infection, and protect the injury while it heals. But implementing these principles requires the right supplies and some basic knowledge.

Adhesive bandages in various sizes handle most minor cuts and scrapes. I carry both standard bandages and some larger ones designed for knees and elbows. The key is having enough bandages for multiple injuries or for changing dressings over several days. During extended emergencies, you might not be able to resupply your first aid kit, so plan accordingly.

Gauze pads and medical tape provide more versatile wound care options than pre-made bandages. You can cut gauze to fit any size wound, and medical tape allows you to secure dressings exactly where you need them. I learned to appreciate this flexibility during a hiking trip when someone in our group got a deep gash on their shin that was too large for any bandage we had. We ended up using gauze and tape to create a custom dressing that worked perfectly.

Antiseptic supplies help prevent infections that can turn minor injuries into serious problems. I carry both antiseptic wipes for cleaning wounds and a small bottle of antiseptic solution for more thorough cleaning. During emergency situations when you might not have access to clean water, having dedicated antiseptic supplies becomes especially important.

Pain relief medication addresses both comfort and function during emergencies. Pain isn't just unpleasant, it can impair your ability to think clearly and perform necessary tasks. I carry both ibuprofen and acetaminophen because they work through different mechanisms and can be more effective when used together for severe pain. Ibuprofen also reduces inflammation, helping with sprains and other soft tissue injuries.

Emergency medications can be lifesavers in specific situations. I keep a few tablets of antihistamine like Benadryl for severe allergic reactions. Aspirin for potential heart attack symptoms (though you should get professional medical help as soon as possible). Anti-diarrheal medication because digestive problems during an emergency evacuation can be both miserable and dangerous.

Elastic bandages help stabilize sprained joints and provide compression for soft tissue injuries. During a day hike in Joshua Tree, someone in our group twisted their ankle badly enough that they couldn't walk normally. An elastic bandage provided enough support that they could walk out under their own power instead of requiring a rescue.

Thermometer helps you monitor for fever, indicating infection or other serious medical problems. Digital thermometers are small, accurate, and battery-powered. Knowing whether someone has a fever helps you make better decisions about whether they need immediate medical attention or can continue with planned activities.

Personal Medications

If you take prescription medications regularly, running out during an emergency can quickly turn a manageable situation into a life-threatening crisis. I learned about the importance of medication planning during my disaster recovery work at Trader Joe's, where we had to consider how employees with medical conditions would manage during extended business disruptions.

The basic rule for emergency medication planning is to always have at least a 30-day supply of critical medications if you can manage it, and a minimum of one week's supply at all times. The full system for building, storing, and maintaining that supply is covered in Chapter 21, which explains why medications deserve their own dedicated kit separate from your bug out bag. The short version: during major disasters, pharmacies might be closed, prescription databases might be offline, and your regular doctor might not be available to write new prescriptions. Having your own supply on hand is the difference between managing and improvising.

Getting extra medication supplies requires some planning and communication with your doctor and pharmacist. Many insurance plans allow early refills if you explain that you're building an emergency kit. Some doctors will write prescriptions for emergency supplies if you explain your preparedness planning. It's worth having this conversation before you need the medications.

Rotation schedules ensure your emergency medications stay fresh and effective. A sixty-day expiration buffer gives you time to replace medications before they actually expire. The full storage and rotation system is in Chapter 21.

Medication documentation helps if you need medical care during an emergency. I keep a written list of all my medications, dosages, and prescribing doctors in my bug out bag. This information can be critical if you're unconscious or confused and can't communicate with emergency medical personnel. Include both prescription and over-the-counter medications you take regularly.

Temperature-sensitive medications require special consideration. Some medications like insulin need refrigeration, obviously not possible in most bug out bag scenarios. If you depend on temperature-sensitive medications, you need to research cooling options like medication cooling cases or plan for very short-term evacuation scenarios where you can reach medical facilities quickly.

Controlled substances present additional challenges because of legal restrictions on how much you can possess at one time. Work with your doctor to understand what's legally possible for emergency supplies, and consider whether there are alternative medications that might be easier to stockpile for emergencies.

Emergency medical information should be easily accessible to anyone who might need to help you during a crisis. I carry a small card in my wallet with critical medical information: medications, allergies, medical conditions, emergency contacts, and my doctor's information. This card could save your life if you're found unconscious after an accident.

Hygiene Supplies

Personal hygiene might seem like a luxury during emergencies, but it's directly connected to health and morale. Poor hygiene can lead to skin infections, dental problems, and other medical issues that complicate an already difficult situation. During extended emergencies, maintaining some basic hygiene routines also helps preserve psychological well-being and the ability to function in social situations.

Water conservation affects all hygiene planning during emergencies. You can't waste precious drinking water on washing when that water might be needed to prevent dehydration. This means choosing hygiene methods that use minimal water or no water at all. I learned this during camping trips in the desert where water was strictly limited and every drop had to be conserved for drinking.

Body wipes designed for camping or military use provide a way to clean yourself without using any water. These wipes are larger and more durable than baby wipes and are designed to remove dirt, sweat, and odor from adult bodies. I keep a package of these in my bug out bag and have used them during power outages when normal bathing wasn't possible. They're not as good as a real shower, but they make a huge difference in comfort and cleanliness.

Dental hygiene becomes especially important during stress because poor oral health can affect your overall health and your ability to eat properly. I carry a travel toothbrush and small tube of toothpaste in my emergency kit. In situations where water is limited, you can brush with just a tiny amount of water or even dry brush to remove plaque and bacteria.

Foot care deserves special attention because foot problems can seriously impair your mobility during emergencies. Blisters, infections, or other foot problems can turn a manageable evacuation into a serious crisis if you can't walk. I learned this during long hiking trips where proper foot care was the difference between enjoying the hike and being miserable for days.

Clean, dry socks are probably the most important foot care item you can carry. I keep several pairs of clean socks in my bug out bag and change them whenever my feet get wet or sweaty. Even if you don't have access to washing facilities, changing into dry socks helps your feet stay healthier and more comfortable.

Feminine hygiene products are essential for women and shouldn't be overlooked in emergency planning. Menstrual periods don't stop for disasters, and not having proper supplies can create both health and dignity issues during already stressful situations. Make sure the women in your household or group have adequate supplies in their emergency kits and that these supplies are rotated regularly.

Hand sanitizer provides a way to kill germs when soap and water aren't available. During emergencies, you might be handling debris, using unfamiliar facilities, or unable to wash your hands properly before eating. Hand sanitizer isn't as effective as proper handwashing, but it's much better than nothing for preventing the spread of germs and disease.

Toilet paper and sanitation supplies address basic human needs that don't disappear during emergencies. Public facilities might be damaged or unavailable, and you might need to create improvised waste disposal solutions. Having your own supplies ensures you can maintain basic sanitation regardless of what facilities are available.

Personal care items that might seem trivial can have outsized effects on morale and psychological well-being. A small mirror, comb, or razor might not be essential for survival, but they can help you maintain a sense of normalcy and self-respect during chaotic situations. The psychological benefits of feeling somewhat clean and presentable shouldn't be underestimated.

Mental Health Considerations

Mental health during emergencies is just as important as physical health, but it gets much less attention in most preparedness planning. Stress, fear, and uncertainty can impair your judgment and decision-making ability when you need them most. I learned this during the Northridge earthquake when the psychological stress of not knowing where our son was affected our ability to think clearly and make good decisions.

Stress management during emergencies starts with understanding that stress reactions are normal and expected. Your body is designed to respond to threats with increased alertness, faster heart rate, and heightened awareness. These responses can be helpful in short-term crisis situations, but they become problematic if they persist for days or weeks without relief.

Sleep deprivation quickly compounds stress and impairs mental function. During the earthquake aftermath, we went more than 24 hours without sleep while searching for our son and dealing with damage to our apartment. By the end of that period, we were making poor decisions and overreacting to minor problems that wouldn't have registered on a normal day. Rest isn't a luxury in an extended emergency. It's what keeps your judgment functional.

Routine and normalcy help maintain psychological stability during chaotic situations. Simple rituals like making coffee in the morning, brushing your teeth before bed, or reading for a few minutes can provide anchors of familiarity when everything else is disrupted. I carry a small book in my bug out bag partly for entertainment but mostly because reading provides a mental escape from stress.

Isolation during extended emergencies is its own problem. Humans aren't wired for extended isolation under stress, and the anxiety and depression that develop can impair judgment faster than most physical threats. If you're with other people, maintaining communication and psychological support matters as much as sharing food and water.

Your brain gets tired from making decisions the same way your legs get tired from walking. Constant survival decisions degrade judgment faster than people expect. A pre-packed bag and a predetermined evacuation plan aren't just convenient -- they reduce the number of decisions you have to make under stress, which means the decisions you do have to make get more of your attention.

Fear management requires acknowledging that fear is normal while not letting it paralyze you. During that forest fire when I thought I was going to die, fear could have caused me to make poor decisions that would have gotten me killed. Instead, I tried to channel the fear into heightened awareness and careful decision-making. Fear can be useful if you don't let it overwhelm your judgment.

Communication with family members helps manage anxiety for everyone involved. During emergencies, not knowing the status of loved ones can be more stressful than dealing with your own immediate problems. Having communication plans and backup methods for staying in touch can reduce anxiety and help everyone make better decisions.

Alcohol and other substances impair the judgment and fine motor control you need most during an emergency. A drink that takes the edge off on a normal evening becomes a liability when you need to think clearly and move precisely. If you regularly use substances to manage stress, plan now for what you'll do instead during an extended emergency.

Post-traumatic stress can develop days or weeks after an emergency, even when you handled the event itself well. It affects your ability to sleep, concentrate, and function normally. Knowing in advance that this is a recognized, treatable response matters -- people who don't know it can happen sometimes interpret the symptoms as personal failure, which makes them worse. Help is available and effective.

Mental preparation through visualization and planning can reduce stress when emergencies occur. I practice evacuation scenarios mentally, thinking through what I would do in different situations and how I would handle various challenges. This mental rehearsal makes emergencies feel more manageable because I've already thought through many of the decisions I might need to make.

Chapter 7: Tools and Equipment

Multi-tools and Knives

A good knife or multi-tool can mean the difference between being able to solve problems and being helpless when things break or need modification. I learned this during that Christmas hike in 1986 when my father and I got trapped in the canyon. When it started getting dark and cold, we needed to cut branches for shelter and warmth, but we had nothing sharper than our house keys. We ended up breaking branches by hand, exhausting work that gave us pieces too big to be useful.

The multi-tool I carry now combines a dozen functions in a package smaller than a smartphone. Pliers for gripping and bending. Wire cutters for electrical work. Multiple knife blades for different cutting tasks. Screwdrivers for equipment repairs. Scissors for precision cutting. A can opener for food. Even a small saw for cutting wood or plastic. Having all these tools in one compact package means I can handle most repair and modification tasks without carrying a full toolbox.

I chose a Leatherman multi-tool after testing several different brands during my hiking days. The build quality is excellent, the tools lock securely when deployed, and the pliers are strong enough for serious work. I've used it to repair broken pack straps, cut firewood, open cans, tighten loose screws on equipment, and perform dozens of other tasks over the years. After a decade of carrying one, I can't imagine packing without it.

The quality of the knife blade matters more than most people realize. Cheap steel won't hold an edge and can even be dangerous if it breaks under stress. During a camping trip in the desert, someone in our group had a bargain multi-tool where the knife blade snapped while they were trying to cut paracord. The broken blade was sharp and jagged, creating a safety hazard instead of solving a problem.

Knife maintenance becomes important when you're depending on a blade for essential tasks. A dull knife is not only ineffective, it's dangerous because you have to use more force and are more likely to slip and cut yourself. I carry a small sharpening stone in my kit and know how to use it properly. Even a few minutes of sharpening can restore a blade's effectiveness when you need it most.

Dedicated knives offer advantages over multi-tool blades for certain tasks. A fixed-blade knife is stronger and more reliable than a folding knife because there are no moving parts to break. The trade-off is size and weight. I carry both a multi-tool and a small fixed-blade knife, giving me versatility for light tasks and reliability for heavy-duty work.

Knife safety becomes critical when you're using blades under stress or in difficult conditions. Always cut away from your body and keep your fingers out of the path of the blade. A sharp knife in experienced hands is much safer than a dull knife in inexperienced hands. If you're not comfortable using knives, practice with safer tasks before you need the skill in an emergency.

Legal considerations affect what knives you can carry in different jurisdictions. Knife laws vary widely between states, counties, and cities. What's legal in rural areas might be illegal in urban areas. Before adding knives to your emergency kit, research the laws in areas where you might travel during an evacuation. Getting arrested for carrying illegal weapons during an emergency would be a disaster on top of a disaster.

Repair and Maintenance Items

Things break during emergencies, often at the worst possible times. Equipment that's been working fine for months suddenly fails when you're depending on it most. I learned this during the Northridge earthquake when several pieces of equipment we thought we could rely on stopped working due to the shaking, moisture, or just the stress of unusual use.

Duct tape has become legendary among outdoor enthusiasts and emergency preparedness people because it can fix almost anything temporarily. I've used duct tape to repair torn gear, seal leaking containers, secure loose equipment, mark trails, and even create emergency bandages. The key word is "temporarily" though. Duct tape is a short-term fix that gets you through an immediate crisis, not a permanent repair.

I wrap several feet of duct tape around my hiking poles or water bottles instead of carrying a whole roll. This saves weight and space while still giving me access to this versatile repair material. Some people wrap duct tape around a pencil or small dowel to create a compact dispenser that's easy to use.

Electrical tape handles repairs that duct tape can't, especially anything involving wires or electrical connections. During a power outage after an ice storm, I used electrical tape to repair a damaged extension cord that was powering our emergency radio. Duct tape wouldn't have provided adequate insulation for the electrical connection.

Cable ties (zip ties) secure things that tape can't handle effectively. They're strong for their size and can bundle cables, secure loose gear, or even create emergency repairs for broken equipment. I learned about their versatility during my computer industry days, where we used them for everything from cable management to emergency equipment repairs.

Super glue fixes things that need more than tape but less than major repairs. Broken plastic equipment, torn fabric, split seams, or cracked containers can often be repaired well enough to remain functional with a small tube of super glue. The key is using it quickly before the crack spreads or the pieces get lost.

Wire for emergency repairs can solve problems that other materials can't address. I carry a small coil of multi-strand wire that's flexible enough to bend repeatedly without breaking but strong enough to secure gear or make electrical connections. During a camping trip, I used wire to repair a broken tent pole by splinting it to a stick, creating a repair that lasted the rest of the trip.

Sewing supplies handle fabric repairs that other materials can't fix properly. A small sewing kit with needles, thread, and a few buttons can repair torn clothing, fix broken straps, or even patch holes in tents or tarps. Learning basic sewing skills before you need them makes these repairs much easier under stress.

Replacement parts for critical equipment can prevent minor failures from becoming major problems. Extra batteries for lights and radios. Spare laces for boots. Replacement water bottle caps. Backup charging cables for electronics. The key is identifying single points of failure in your equipment and carrying backups for the most critical ones.

Fire Starting Equipment

Fire provides warmth, light, the ability to cook food, water purification through boiling, and psychological comfort during stressful situations. But starting fires can be challenging under emergency conditions when you're cold, wet, stressed, or dealing with poor weather. I learned this during winter camping trips where fire starting became a survival skill instead of a convenience.

Redundancy in fire starting methods is essential because any single method can fail when you need it most. I carry multiple ways to create fire: waterproof matches, a reliable lighter, a ferro rod (fire steel), and even some fire cubes as backup tinder. This might seem like overkill, but fire is too important to risk having only one option.

Waterproof matches solve the most common fire starting problem: wet ignition sources. Regular matches become useless if they get damp, something that can happen even in sealed containers if humidity gets in. Waterproof matches will light even after being submerged in water, though they cost more than regular matches.

Lighters provide an easy, reliable ignition source that works in most conditions. I carry a basic Bic lighter because they're dependable, inexpensive, and work thousands of times before the fuel runs out. The downside is that lighters can fail at high altitude, in extreme cold, or if they get wet. They also run out of fuel eventually.

Ferro rods create sparks hot enough to ignite tinder even when wet. These fire steels work by scraping them with a metal striker to produce a shower of molten iron sparks. They don't depend on fuel or chemical igniters, so they work in conditions that defeat matches and lighters. The downside is that they require practice to use effectively and good tinder to catch the sparks.

I learned to use a ferro rod during CERT training where we practiced fire starting under difficult conditions. It takes practice to get the technique right, but once you learn it, ferro rods are reliable. They work when they're wet, at any altitude, and in extreme temperatures. A good ferro rod will provide thousands of fires.

Tinder preparation is often overlooked but important for successful fire starting. Tinder is the fine, dry material that catches your initial spark or flame and burns hot enough to ignite kindling. Good natural tinder includes dry grass, birch bark, pine needles, or wood shavings. Man-made tinder like petroleum jelly-soaked cotton balls or commercial fire cubes lights easily and burns hot.

I carry both natural and artificial tinder in my fire starting kit. The artificial tinder is guaranteed to work even in wet conditions, while natural tinder is available anywhere there's vegetation. During winter conditions or in wet climates, having reliable artificial tinder can be the difference between getting a fire started and staying cold.

Fire building technique matters as much as having good ignition sources and tinder. You need to progress from tinder to kindling (pencil-thin dry wood) to fuel wood (thumb-thick and larger) in a controlled progression. Trying to jump from a small flame directly to large pieces of wood usually results in the fire going out.

Safety considerations become critical when you're building fires during emergency conditions. Clear the area around your fire of flammable materials. Have water available to extinguish the fire completely when you're done. Never leave a fire unattended. During my forest fire experience, I saw firsthand how quickly fires can spread under the right conditions.

Cordage and Fasteners

Rope, cord, and fasteners solve an amazing variety of problems during emergency situations. Securing loose gear. Creating shelter. Making repairs. Bundling supplies. Marking routes. Even creating emergency rescue systems. I learned about the importance of good cordage during my hiking days when having the right rope or cord often meant the difference between a successful trip and a miserable experience.

Paracord has become the gold standard for emergency cordage because it combines strength, versatility, and compact storage. True military-specification paracord is rated for 550 pounds of tensile strength, hence the nickname "550 cord." Inside the outer sheath are seven inner strands that can be removed and used separately for lighter-duty tasks like fishing line or sewing thread.

I carry about 50 feet of paracord in my bug out bag, enough for most emergency applications without taking up excessive space or weight. I've used paracord to secure tarps, hang food away from animals, repair broken equipment, create emergency shelters, and even make improvised repairs to vehicle parts during breakdowns.

The quality of paracord varies enormously, and cheap imitations can be dangerous if you're depending on them for critical applications. Real military-spec paracord has specific construction standards and strength ratings. Cheap "paracord" might look similar but use inferior materials that break under much lower loads than advertised.

Different weights of cordage serve different purposes. Heavy paracord for structural applications and major repairs. Lighter utility cord for bundling gear and moderate-duty tasks. Thin cord or even string for light repairs and detailed work. Having a variety of cord weights gives you options for different situations.

Carabiners provide quick, reliable connection points for ropes and gear. These metal clips can secure equipment, create anchor points for shelters, or connect multiple pieces of gear together. I carry several small carabiners because they're lightweight and useful for organizing and securing equipment.

Bungee cords excel at securing loads that need to compress or accommodate movement. Traditional rope holds things firmly in place, but bungee cords can absorb shock and vibration while maintaining tension. During vehicle evacuations, bungee cords can secure loose gear that would be difficult to tie down with regular rope.

Knot knowledge becomes important when you're using cordage for emergency applications. A few basic knots can handle most situations: bowline for creating a loop that won't slip, clove hitch for securing rope to posts or poles, and trucker's hitch for creating mechanical advantage when tightening rope. Practice these knots until you can tie them in the dark.

Fasteners like safety pins, clips, and small buckles solve problems that rope can't address effectively. Safety pins can repair torn clothing or gear, create emergency fasteners, or even serve as fish hooks in survival situations. Small clips can secure lightweight items without the bulk of rope or cord.

Cutting tools for cordage maintenance ensure you can modify and repair your rope and cord when needed. A sharp knife can cut rope cleanly without fraying the ends. Some multi-tools include wire cutters that work well for cutting small cord. Heat-sealing synthetic rope ends prevents fraying and extends the useful life of your cordage.

Storage and organization of cordage prevents tangling and makes it accessible when needed. Rope stored loose in a pack will inevitably become a tangled mess when you need it quickly. I coil rope properly and secure it with rubber bands or small ties. Some people prefer rope storage bags that keep everything organized and ready to use.

Chapter 8: Documentation and Information

Essential Documents

When disaster strikes, you might need to prove who you are, where you live, what you own, and what insurance coverage you have. I learned this during the aftermath of the Northridge earthquake when we needed to file insurance claims but couldn't find half our important documents in the chaos of our damaged apartment. What should have been a simple process turned into weeks of phone calls and bureaucratic hassles while we tried to reconstruct our records.

The documents you need during emergencies fall into several categories, and losing access to any of them can create serious problems. Identity documents prove who you are and allow you to access services, cross borders, or get help from authorities. Financial documents let you access money, prove what you own, and file insurance claims. Medical documents ensure you get proper treatment and can obtain prescription medications.

Personal identification forms the foundation of all other documentation: driver's license or state ID card, passport, Social Security card, and birth certificate establish your identity and citizenship. During evacuations, you might need to cross state lines or prove your identity to authorities. I keep copies of these documents in my bug out bag and originals in a fireproof safe at home.

Insurance documentation becomes critical when you need to file claims for damaged or destroyed property. Homeowner's or renter's insurance policies, auto insurance, health insurance cards, and life insurance policies all contain information you'll need to access benefits. The policy numbers, contact information, and coverage details are essential for getting help quickly after a disaster.

I learned about insurance documentation importance during my disaster recovery work at Trader Joe's. We maintained detailed records of all company insurance policies and kept copies in multiple locations. When facilities were damaged, having immediate access to policy information meant we could start the claims process within hours instead of days or weeks.

Financial account information helps you access money when normal banking might be disrupted. Bank account numbers, credit card information, investment account details, and loan documentation can all become important if you need to access funds or prove financial status during extended emergencies. During major disasters, bank computer systems might be offline for days.

Medical records and prescription information ensure you can get proper healthcare when your regular providers aren't available. Medical history, current medications, allergies, and emergency contacts help unfamiliar medical personnel treat you safely and effectively. During the stress of emergencies, people often forget important medical details that could affect their treatment.

Property documentation proves what you own and helps with insurance claims and replacement purchases. Deeds, titles, appraisals, and receipts for valuable items establish ownership and value. Taking photographs or video of your property before disasters strike provides visual documentation that insurance companies accept for claims processing.

Legal documents protect your interests and those of your family members. Wills, power of attorney designations, guardianship papers, and other legal instruments ensure that your wishes are carried out if you're incapacitated or killed during an emergency. These documents also help family members access your accounts and make decisions on your behalf.

Contact information for professionals who help you manage your affairs becomes essential when you need to reach them during emergencies: phone numbers and addresses for your doctor, lawyer, accountant, insurance agent, and financial advisor. During chaotic post-disaster periods, having this information readily available can save enormous amounts of time and stress.

Digital Storage Solutions

Technology has revolutionized how we can store and access important documents, but it also creates new vulnerabilities. Digital storage offers advantages like compact size, easy copying, and remote access, but it depends on having power, working devices, and network connectivity. I learned to balance digital convenience with analog reliability after experiencing various technology failures during emergencies.

Cloud storage services provide the ultimate backup for important documents because the information is stored on servers in multiple locations far from your home. Services like Google Drive, Dropbox, or iCloud let you upload scanned copies of documents that you can access from any device with internet connectivity. During Hurricane Sandy, people who had documents in cloud storage could access them even when their homes were destroyed.

The downside of cloud storage is that it requires internet access, which might not be available during emergencies. Cell towers can be damaged, internet infrastructure can fail, and your devices might run out of power. This is why cloud storage should supplement, not replace, physical document storage.

Encrypted storage becomes important when you're putting sensitive information in digital formats. Documents containing Social Security numbers, account information, and other personal data need protection from identity thieves and hackers. I use encrypted cloud storage and password-protected files for sensitive documents. Even if someone gains access to my storage, they can't read the documents without the encryption keys.

Local digital storage provides a compromise between cloud convenience and offline reliability. USB drives, external hard drives, or even old smartphones can store digital copies of important documents that don't depend on internet connectivity. I keep an encrypted USB drive in my bug out bag with copies of essential documents that I can access from any computer.

Multiple device backup ensures you can access information even if one device fails. Having document copies on your phone, laptop, tablet, and external storage means you're not dependent on any single device working properly. During the Northridge earthquake, some people lost all their information because it was stored on only one computer that was damaged.

File organization systems help you find information quickly when you're stressed and working with unfamiliar devices. I organize digital documents into clearly labeled folders with descriptive file names. "Insurance_Homeowners_Policy_2026.pdf" is much more useful than "Document1.pdf" when you're trying to find information under pressure.

Regular updates keep your digital document collection current and useful. Insurance policies change, bank accounts get closed, new medical conditions develop, and contact information becomes outdated. I review and update my digital document collection every six months, adding new documents and removing obsolete ones.

Test your backup systems periodically from a device you don't normally use. I've found corrupted files and expired login credentials during routine checks that would have been serious problems during an actual emergency. The test takes ten minutes. The discovery during a crisis takes hours you don't have.

Emergency Contacts

Having the right contact information readily available can be the difference between getting help quickly and being stuck without assistance during emergencies. But contact information becomes useless if you can't access it when networks are down or devices are damaged. I learned this during the earthquake when our address book was buried under debris and we couldn't remember important phone numbers that weren't stored in our (broken) cell phones.

Family contact information forms the core of any emergency contact system: phone numbers, addresses, and email addresses for immediate family members, close relatives, and anyone who might be caring for children or elderly family members. During disasters, families often get separated, and having multiple ways to reach each other becomes critical for coordination and peace of mind.

Out-of-area contacts often work better than local contacts during regional disasters. When local phone networks are overloaded or damaged, long-distance calls sometimes get through when local calls don't. I learned this during CERT training where we practiced using distant relatives as communication hubs for coordinating local family members.

Medical contacts ensure you can get healthcare when your regular providers aren't available: phone numbers for your primary doctor, specialists, pharmacy, and medical insurance company. Hospital contact information for facilities in areas where you might evacuate. Emergency medical services and poison control numbers that work from anywhere.

Professional service contacts help you deal with property damage and insurance claims: contact information for your insurance agent, lawyer, accountant, bank, and any contractors who work on your property. During post-disaster recovery, you'll need to coordinate with these people to assess damage, file claims, and arrange repairs.

Utility company contacts help you report outages and get service restored: phone numbers for electric, gas, water, sewer, internet, and cable companies. Many utility companies have separate numbers for emergency reporting that get priority handling during major outages. Knowing these numbers can help you get service restored faster.

Government agency contacts provide access to official information and assistance programs: local emergency management office, police and fire departments, health department, and social services. During major disasters, these agencies coordinate relief efforts and can provide information about shelters, food distribution, and other assistance programs.

Multiple contact methods increase your chances of reaching people when primary communication channels fail: phone numbers, email addresses, social media accounts, and even physical addresses for important contacts. During Hurricane Sandy, some people communicated through Facebook when phone networks were down.

Redundant storage ensures you can access contact information even if your primary storage is lost or damaged. I keep contact information in my phone, written on paper in my wallet, stored digitally in cloud services, and memorized for the most critical numbers. This redundancy means I can always reach important people regardless of what equipment I have available.

Important Information Management

Managing important information during emergencies requires balancing accessibility with security. You need information to be readily available when you need it, but you also need to protect sensitive data from theft or misuse. I developed my approach to information management through trial and error during various emergencies and preparedness exercises.

Not all information carries equal weight during an emergency. Identity documents and medical records are immediately life-critical. Insurance and financial records matter for recovery but not survival. Entertainment and convenience data can wait indefinitely. Knowing which tier each item falls into keeps you from wasting time during a crisis.

I organize information into three tiers: immediate survival, short-term recovery, and long-term rebuilding. Immediate survival information stays most accessible and includes medical conditions, emergency contacts, and basic identification. Short-term recovery information includes insurance policies and financial accounts. Long-term rebuilding information includes property documentation and professional contacts.

Physical backup systems provide information access when digital systems fail: important phone numbers written on waterproof paper and stored in your wallet, key account numbers and contact information on laminated cards, critical medical information on medical alert bracelets or cards. These analog backups work regardless of power, network connectivity, or device failures.

During an emergency you may need to access your bank account, insurance website, or cloud storage from a borrowed phone or public computer. If your passwords exist only in your head or in an app on a device you no longer have, you're locked out. A password manager with cloud sync and a memorized master password solves this. A written backup of critical passwords in your emergency kit solves it when the internet is down.

I use a password manager that stores encrypted passwords in cloud storage and can be accessed from any device with internet connectivity. The master password is something I've memorized, and I keep a backup of critical passwords written down and stored securely. This system lets me access important accounts even when I don't have my usual devices.

Information sharing protocols help family members access important information when you're not available. If you're injured or separated during an emergency, other family members might need to access your accounts or information to handle critical tasks. This requires balancing security with accessibility and having clear procedures for emergency information sharing.

Contact information goes stale faster than most people expect. Bank accounts close, doctors retire, insurance policies renew under different terms. I go through my digital document collection every six months, update what's changed, and pull anything that no longer reflects my actual situation.

Physical documents go in a fireproof container. Digital copies get encrypted and password protected. Backup copies live in separate locations so no single disaster takes everything. The harder design problem is making sure family members can actually access this during an emergency without the information being freely accessible all the time. A shared secure note with instructions, opened to the right people, is usually the practical answer.

If both your primary and backup systems are lost, recovery means contacting each institution individually for replacement documents, going through credit agencies to verify your identity without standard documentation, and proving eligibility for services with whatever you have. It's slow and bureaucratic. The shortcut is knowing which institutions you'd contact and in what order before you ever need to.

Verify periodically that family members know how to access shared information, and that backup systems contain current data rather than documents from three years ago that no longer reflect your accounts, insurance policies, or contact information. The worst time to discover your emergency documents are out of date is when you're standing in front of someone who needs to see them.

Chapter 9: Personal Security

Situational Awareness

Personal security starts with awareness of your surroundings and the ability to recognize potential threats before they become immediate dangers. I learned this during the chaos following the Northridge earthquake when normal social structures broke down and some people took advantage of the confusion to commit crimes. Being aware of what was happening around me became just as important as having emergency supplies.

Situational awareness isn't paranoia or constant fear, it's simply paying attention to your environment and the people in it. During normal times, most of us walk around in a mental fog, focused on our phones, our thoughts, or our daily routines. We tune out most of what's happening around us because our brains filter out information that doesn't seem immediately relevant. But during emergencies, that filtered-out information can be critical for your safety.

The baseline concept helps you recognize when something is wrong by first understanding what normal looks like in any given environment. During my CERT training, we practiced establishing baselines for different locations: what does a normal neighborhood look like during the day versus at night, what kinds of people are usually in a particular area, what sounds and activities are typical. Once you know what normal looks like, deviations from that baseline become much more obvious.

I learned to apply this during the forest fire evacuation when I was trapped on the mountain road. The baseline for that area was light traffic and peaceful mountain scenery. When I started seeing emergency vehicles, smoke, and panicked drivers, it was clear that something was seriously wrong even before I could see the fire. Recognizing the deviation from baseline gave me time to prepare mentally for what was coming.

Trust your instincts when something feels wrong, even if you can't articulate exactly what's bothering you. Your subconscious mind processes much more information than your conscious mind and can pick up on subtle cues that indicate danger. During emergencies, when stress levels are high and normal social controls may be weakened, these instincts become even more important.

I experienced this during the earthquake aftermath when we were walking through damaged areas looking for our son. Several times I felt uncomfortable in certain areas even though I couldn't point to anything wrong. Later, we learned that some of those areas had experienced looting and other criminal activity. My gut feeling had picked up on subtle signs that my conscious mind hadn't processed.

When you walk into any space, note where the exits are and what's between you and them. Identify anything heavy or rigid within reach. Figure out where you'd go if someone came through the door doing harm. This sounds like paranoia described on paper and feels like nothing in practice. Within a few weeks it becomes a habit you run automatically, like checking your mirrors when you drive.

The tell is behavior that doesn't match the environment. Someone dressed wrong for the weather. Someone who's watching other people instead of doing whatever they came to do. Someone moving against the flow of foot traffic. During disasters these signals matter more because normal social inhibitions are lowered and help can be hard to get quickly. Most people approaching you want the same things you do. A few don't, and the ones who don't usually advertise it if you're paying attention.

Your phone is a tracking device you carry voluntarily. During an emergency, that's mostly fine and sometimes critical. But cell phones can be tracked, social media posts broadcast your location to anyone watching, and card payments leave a trail. Know this and make conscious choices about what you post and when.

Personal Protection Items

Personal protection during emergencies requires balancing the need for safety with legal restrictions and practical considerations. You want to be able to defend yourself if necessary, but you also need to avoid carrying items that could get you in legal trouble or that you're not trained to use effectively. I learned about this balance through my emergency response training and unfortunately through some real-world experiences during disasters.

Pepper spray offers effective personal protection that's legal in most jurisdictions and doesn't require extensive training to use safely. During the chaotic period after the earthquake, my wife started carrying pepper spray when she had to walk through damaged areas alone. It gave her confidence and a means of protection that she could use effectively without years of martial arts training.

The key with pepper spray is getting a quality product and understanding its limitations. Cheap pepper spray can malfunction when you need it most, and all pepper spray has limited range and can be affected by wind conditions. I keep a small canister in my bug out bag and have tested it (outdoors) to understand how it works and what to expect. You don't want your first experience with pepper spray to be during an emergency.

Personal alarms create loud noises that can deter attackers and attract help. These small devices are completely legal everywhere and can be effective in situations where other people are nearby who might respond to the alarm. During disasters when police response times might be extended, having a way to attract attention can be valuable.

Tactical pens provide a discreet self-defense option that doubles as a useful tool. These are sturdy pens designed to be used as impact weapons if necessary. They're legal to carry anywhere that allows pens, which is virtually everywhere. I carry one as my everyday writing instrument, so it's always available without looking like a weapon.

Flashlights serve double duty as illumination tools and potential defensive weapons. A heavy, bright flashlight can temporarily blind an attacker and can be used as an impact weapon if necessary. The advantage is that flashlights are obviously useful tools that no one questions you carrying, unlike items that are clearly designed as weapons.

Self-defense training is more valuable than any weapon you can carry. Knowing how to fight back effectively, how to escape from grabs and holds, and how to use improvised weapons gives you options regardless of what equipment you have available. During my disaster preparedness training, we learned basic self-defense techniques that focused on escaping instead of fighting.

Avoidance remains the best personal protection strategy. Don't go places that seem dangerous. Don't display valuable items that might attract criminals. Stay with groups when possible instead of traveling alone. Trust your instincts when someone or someplace feels wrong. Most criminal activity during disasters is opportunistic, and criminals generally prefer easy targets.

Legal considerations vary dramatically between jurisdictions, and what's legal in one place might be a felony in another. Research the laws in your area and any places you might travel during an evacuation. Getting arrested for carrying illegal weapons during an emergency would create a whole new set of problems when you're already dealing with a crisis.

Cash and Valuables

Electronic payment systems can fail during emergencies, leaving you unable to buy necessities if you don't have cash. I learned this during a regional power outage that lasted several days after an ice storm. Credit card readers didn't work, ATMs were offline, and even stores that were open could only accept cash payments. Having physical money became the difference between being able to buy supplies and going without.

Cash amounts in your bug out bag should be substantial enough to handle real emergencies but not so large that losing the bag would be financially devastating. I keep about $500 in small bills in my emergency kit, hidden in multiple locations throughout the bag. This is enough to buy food, fuel, and basic supplies for several days but not enough to ruin me financially if the bag is lost or stolen.

Small bill denominations are important because during emergencies, people might not be able to make change for large bills. Having twenties, tens, fives, and ones gives you flexibility when making purchases. I learned this during a disaster response exercise where local businesses were simulating post-disaster conditions. People with hundred-dollar bills couldn't buy anything because no one could make change.

Hidden storage locations protect your cash from casual theft while keeping it accessible when you need it. I keep some money in an obvious wallet as "mugger money" that can be handed over if threatened, while the real emergency cash is hidden in various pockets and compartments throughout my gear. If someone steals my wallet, I still have access to most of my emergency funds.

Foreign currency might be useful if you live near international borders or if disasters affect banking systems broadly enough to undermine confidence in local currency. During some historical disasters, foreign currency has been more trusted than local money. This is probably overkill for most people, but if you live near Mexico or Canada, having some foreign cash might provide additional options.

Precious metals like gold or silver coins offer value storage that doesn't depend on financial systems, but they're heavy, can be difficult to spend, and might attract unwanted attention. I don't carry precious metals in my bug out bag because the disadvantages outweigh the benefits for short-term emergencies. They're better suited for long-term economic collapse scenarios than 72-hour evacuations.

Valuable documents like titles, deeds, and certificates need protection from theft as well as damage. These documents can be replaced, but the process is time-consuming and bureaucratic. I keep copies in my bug out bag but store originals in a bank safe deposit box or fireproof safe at home.

Jewelry and personal valuables present a dilemma during emergencies. Sentimental items might be irreplaceable, but they can also make you a target for criminals. If you do carry valuables, keep them small, personally meaningful, and difficult for a thief to identify as worth taking.

Barter items might become useful during extended emergencies when normal commerce breaks down. Cigarettes, alcohol, batteries, and ammunition have historically been valuable trade goods during disasters. I don't smoke or drink, but I keep a small supply of these items because they're compact, store well, and could be useful for trading with people who have things I need.

Identity Protection

Identity theft becomes a greater risk during disasters when normal security procedures break down and people are forced to provide personal information to unfamiliar organizations. I learned about this risk during my disaster recovery work when we had to help employees who had been victims of identity theft after providing personal information to fake relief organizations.

Document security starts with limiting what personal information you carry and protecting what you must have with you. I keep copies of essential documents in my bug out bag instead of originals whenever possible. The copies provide the information I need for most purposes while limiting the damage if they're lost or stolen.

Scam awareness becomes critical when you're dealing with insurance companies, relief organizations, and contractors during disaster recovery. Criminals often pose as legitimate organizations to steal personal information or money from disaster victims. Real relief organizations and insurance companies have procedures and identification. When in doubt, verify independently before providing sensitive information.

I experienced this firsthand after the earthquake when someone called claiming to be from our insurance company and asking for our Social Security numbers and bank account information to "expedite our claim." Something felt wrong about the call, so I hung up and called our insurance company directly. They confirmed that they hadn't called us and wouldn't ask for that information over the phone.

Social media discretion protects you from criminals who monitor social networks for information about people who are away from home or in vulnerable situations. Posting about evacuations, damage to your property, or your current location can make you a target for burglary or other crimes. Save the social media updates for after you're safe and back home.

Credit monitoring becomes important after disasters because identity thieves often target disaster victims. Consider placing fraud alerts on your credit reports if you've had to provide personal information to multiple organizations during disaster recovery. Monitor your credit reports and bank statements carefully for several months after any emergency.

Physical security of devices protects the personal information stored on phones, laptops, and other electronics. Use strong passwords or biometric locks on all devices. Enable remote wipe capabilities that let you erase devices if they're lost or stolen. During emergencies when you might be staying in shelters or other temporary accommodations, device security becomes even more important.

Paper trail management means being careful about what documents you throw away and how you dispose of them. Shred anything with personal information instead of just throwing it in the trash. During disasters when normal trash collection might be disrupted, be especially careful about leaving personal documents where others might find them.

Ask for identification from anyone requesting your personal information during disaster recovery. Verify credentials independently by looking up the organization's phone number yourself and calling it, not by calling the number they give you. Legitimate relief organizations and insurance companies have procedures and won't pressure you to hand over sensitive information on the spot. I hung up on a caller claiming to be from my insurance company after the earthquake and called the number on my policy. They hadn't called me.

If your identity gets stolen during or after an emergency, the response is the same as any other time: fraud alert at the credit bureaus within 24 hours, freeze on your credit, and calls to any financial institution where you saw unauthorized activity. Keep those contact numbers with your emergency documents so you're not searching for them while you're already dealing with a crisis.

Chapter 10: Special Considerations

Family and Pet Preparations

Preparing bug out bags for families requires thinking beyond your own needs to consider the requirements of children, elderly family members, and pets. I learned this during my disaster recovery work at Trader Joe's when we had to consider how our emergency plans would affect employees with families. What works for a single adult in good health doesn't necessarily work for a family with young children or elderly relatives.

Children's needs change dramatically based on their age, and what a toddler requires is completely different from what a teenager needs. During the Northridge earthquake, I watched families struggle because they'd planned for adults but hadn't considered how children would handle the stress, disruption, and physical demands of an emergency evacuation. Kids get scared, tired, hungry, and overwhelmed much faster than adults, and they don't understand why normal routines have been disrupted.

Infant and toddler preparations require the most equipment and supplies. Diapers, baby food, formula, bottles, pacifiers, and comfort items like stuffed animals or blankets become essential when you can't just run to the store. I've seen families have to abandon evacuation plans because they didn't have adequate supplies for their babies. A screaming, hungry infant makes it impossible to move quietly or quickly when necessary.

The challenge with baby supplies is that they're bulky, heavy, and have short shelf lives. Formula expires, diapers get outgrown, and babies' needs change rapidly as they develop. This means family emergency supplies require more frequent updates and rotation than adult supplies. You can't just pack a bag and forget about it for six months.

School-age children need different considerations. They're old enough to carry some of their own supplies but still need adult supervision and support. During evacuations, kids this age often struggle with leaving familiar surroundings and not understanding when they'll be able to return home. Having familiar items like favorite books, games, or comfort objects can help maintain some psychological stability.

I learned about the importance of psychological comfort items during a CERT training exercise where we simulated family evacuations. The children who had brought familiar objects handled the stress much better than those who didn't. Sometimes a small toy or book that weighs almost nothing can make the difference between a cooperative child and one who's having a complete meltdown.

Elderly family members present different challenges, often related to mobility, medications, and medical equipment. During the forest fire evacuation that trapped me on the mountain, I saw elderly people who couldn't walk long distances and families who had to abandon vehicles because grandparents couldn't manage rough terrain. Physical limitations that aren't problems during normal times become serious obstacles during emergency evacuations.

Medication management becomes critical for elderly family members who often take multiple prescription drugs on complex schedules. Unlike younger adults who might be able to skip medications for a day or two, elderly people may have life-threatening conditions that require consistent medication. This means carrying larger supplies of more medications and having better organization systems to manage complex drug regimens.

Pet preparations require thinking like a pet owner, not just a human survivor. Pets can't understand what's happening during emergencies, they can't carry their own supplies, and they can't adapt to new foods or environments as easily as humans. During disasters, pets often become stressed and may behave unpredictably, even if they're normally well-behaved.

Food and water for pets add weight and bulk to emergency supplies, especially for large dogs. A 70-pound dog needs about a gallon of water per day, just like a human. Pet food is heavy, takes up space, and many pets won't eat unfamiliar brands when they're already stressed from the emergency situation.

Keep several days' worth of your pets' regular food in your emergency supplies and rotate it regularly.

Carriers, leashes, and restraint equipment become essential for controlling pets during chaotic evacuations. Even well-trained pets may bolt when they're scared, and losing a pet during an emergency evacuation adds emotional trauma to an already difficult situation. I learned this from neighbors during the earthquake who spent days searching for pets that had fled during the chaos.

Legal documentation for pets includes vaccination records, ownership papers, and identification tags with current contact information. Many emergency shelters and hotels that accept evacuees won't take pets without proof of current vaccinations. Having this paperwork readily available can mean the difference between keeping your pet with you and having to surrender them to animal control.

Seasonal Adjustments

Your bug out bag needs change dramatically based on the season and local climate conditions. What works during a mild spring evacuation could be completely inadequate during a winter storm or summer heat wave. I learned this during my hiking days when I discovered that gear that was perfect for one season could be useless or even dangerous in different weather conditions.

Winter preparations require completely different approaches to clothing, shelter, and heating. During cold weather emergencies, hypothermia becomes a serious threat that can kill you faster than dehydration or hunger. The clothing that keeps you warm during a normal winter day might be inadequate if you're stuck outside overnight or if you're walking long distances in snow and wind.

Layering systems become critical during winter emergencies because your activity level and the weather conditions can change rapidly. Base layers that wick moisture away from your skin, insulating layers that trap warm air, and outer layers that block wind and precipitation. I learned about layering during winter camping trips where the temperature could swing 30 degrees between day and night.

Emergency heat sources take on life-or-death importance during winter conditions. Chemical hand warmers, emergency blankets, and portable heating devices can prevent hypothermia when other heat sources aren't available. During an ice storm that knocked out power for several days, these small heat sources made the difference between being uncomfortable and being in real danger.

Summer preparations focus on different priorities: staying cool, preventing dehydration, and protecting yourself from sun exposure. Heat exhaustion and heat stroke can be just as dangerous as hypothermia, and they can develop much more quickly. During my desert hiking days, I learned that hot weather emergencies can incapacitate you in hours instead of days.

Sun protection becomes critical during summer evacuations when you might be outdoors for extended periods without shade. Sunscreen, hats, and light-colored clothing that covers your skin can prevent burns that would make an already difficult situation much worse. Severe sunburn can prevent your body from cooling properly, increasing the risk of heat-related illness.

Cooling strategies for summer emergencies might include wet bandanas, electrolyte replacement drinks, and understanding how to find or create shade. During hot weather, physical activity needs to be limited to early morning and evening hours when possible. I learned this during desert travel where hiking during midday heat was not just uncomfortable, it was dangerous.

Spring and fall transitions present unique challenges because weather can change rapidly and unpredictably. A warm spring day can turn into a cold, wet nightmare if storms move through. Fall weather can swing from pleasant to freezing in a matter of hours. Emergency preparations during these seasons need to account for worst-case weather scenarios, not average conditions.

Clothing adjustments for transitional seasons mean carrying gear for both warm and cold conditions, adding weight and bulk to your emergency supplies. I learned to focus on versatile pieces that could work in multiple conditions instead of carrying gear for every possible scenario. A good rain jacket, warm hat, and insulating layer can handle most spring and fall weather emergencies.

Regional Considerations

Where you live determines what will kill you in an emergency. The threat profile, the climate, the terrain, the infrastructure, and the available resources are all shaped by geography in ways that generic preparedness advice can't address. I've lived in Southern California earthquake country for most of my adult life and now live in Florida hurricane country, and the differences in how I prepare for emergencies between those two places are substantial enough that the bag I kept in Northridge would have been dangerously wrong for Milton. This section is longer than most because regional adaptation isn't a footnote, it's a core principle.

Florida and the Gulf Coast

Florida is one of the most demanding emergency preparedness environments in the country, and most people moving there from other states dramatically underestimate it until they survive their first major storm. I made that mistake myself when I relocated from California. My earthquake kit was organized and functional, but it was wrong for Florida in almost every dimension.

Hurricane season runs from June 1 through November 30, which means six months of every year require active preparedness posture. This isn't a once-a-decade risk like a major California earthquake, it's an annual operational reality. The correct mindset is not "if a hurricane comes" but "when the next one comes." Supplies should be restocked and checked at the start of each season, not when a storm appears on radar.

The surge map is the most important document a Florida resident can study. Storm surge, not wind, kills most hurricane victims. The surge maps published by the National Hurricane Center show exactly which zones flood at which storm intensities, and they are specific down to individual neighborhoods. Know your zone. Know your zone's history. If you are in Zone A or B and a major storm is approaching, the evacuation decision should be made before the order comes, not after, because the highways that leave the peninsula fill up faster than most people expect. During Milton, I watched neighbors who waited for the official order sit in traffic for eight hours trying to reach destinations that people who left a day earlier reached in two.

Waterproofing everything is non-negotiable in Florida. The humidity alone degrades electronics, medications, and food faster than in any other region I've lived in. Every item in your emergency storage should be in a sealed waterproof container or bag. I use dry bags inside my main pack and keep medications and electronics in small waterproof cases. This is not caution, it is routine maintenance against an environment that corrodes and molds aggressively year-round, not just during storms.

Heat and extended power outages combine into a specific Florida threat that people from cooler climates don't fully grasp until they experience it. After Milton I had five days without power in weather that reached the mid-eighties indoors by mid-morning. No air conditioning in Florida in October is genuinely dangerous for elderly residents and anyone with cardiovascular conditions, not merely uncomfortable. Battery-powered fans, cooling towels, and a plan to reach a cooling center or air-conditioned location if internal temperatures become dangerous are essential components of a Florida emergency kit that would be irrelevant in Minnesota. Know where your county's cooling centers are before you need them.

Insects and wildlife become a more serious concern during and after Florida storms than most emergency guides acknowledge. Standing water after storms breeds mosquitoes within days, and mosquito-borne illness is a real post-hurricane risk. DEET-based repellent and clothing that covers skin belong in every Florida emergency kit. Displaced wildlife, including snakes, is common during floods. Wear boots when walking through flooded or debris-covered areas. I watched a water moccasin cross a parking lot at my complex two days after Milton, displaced by flooded habitat nearby.

Fuel is the logistics problem that collapses Florida evacuations. Gas stations along evacuation routes run out within hours of a major evacuation order. Keep your vehicle above half a tank during hurricane season at all times, not just when a storm appears. If you have a generator, store properly treated fuel before the season begins. During Milton the gas lines at open stations stretched for two to three hours even days after the storm passed, as people tried to fuel generators for extended outages. I had stored fuel and didn't wait in a single line.

The Gulf Coast from the Florida panhandle through Louisiana faces all of the above plus the specific geography of extremely flat coastal terrain with limited high ground. Storm surge from a major Gulf storm can travel miles inland with almost no natural barriers to slow it. Evacuation routes in these areas require more advance planning because they funnel large populations through limited road networks in low-lying terrain. If you live in coastal Louisiana, Mississippi, or Alabama, your evacuation destination needs to be genuinely inland, not just twenty miles from the coast.

California Earthquake Country

The fundamental difference between earthquake preparedness and every other regional preparedness is zero warning time. You go from normal life to full emergency in the time it takes the shaking to reach you. This shapes everything about how you prepare. There is no monitoring a storm track, no watching a forecast, no gradual escalation of threat level. The earthquake hits, and then you deal with what happened.

The Northridge earthquake at 4:31 AM on January 17, 1994 is the event that calibrated all my thinking about preparedness. In the seconds it lasted, furniture became projectiles, gas lines cracked, chimneys collapsed, and the power grid went down across a wide area. Our apartment survived structurally, but the building across the street did not. The people who did best in the immediate aftermath were those who had supplies they could access in the dark while the building was still shaking, not people who had organized kits in hard-to-reach closets.

Furniture anchoring and home hardening belong in an earthquake preparedness plan in a way that doesn't apply elsewhere. Tall bookshelves, water heaters, refrigerators, and heavy furniture should be strapped to wall studs. Cabinet latches prevent dishes and supplies from becoming dangerous debris. Shoes next to the bed prevent foot injuries from broken glass. A flashlight within arm's reach of where you sleep is not optional. These pre-earthquake steps cost very little and prevent the injuries and supply access problems that follow the shaking.

Gas shutoff is a California-specific skill worth learning before an earthquake. The flexible gas lines used in most California homes are earthquake-resistant, but older rigid connections can crack. Know where your gas shutoff is and keep a wrench near it. The fires that follow earthquakes are often more destructive than the shaking itself. Knowing how and when to shut off your gas, and understanding that you should only do so if you smell gas or suspect a leak, can prevent post-earthquake fire from destroying what the shaking left intact.

California wildfire has become a separate and increasingly serious threat layer on top of earthquake risk. The fire seasons have grown longer and more destructive, affecting areas that were historically considered safe. The Lake Arrowhead fire that trapped me on the mountain road, the fires that destroyed Paradise, the Eaton and Palisades fires, and dozens of others demonstrate that urban interface fires now move faster than evacuation systems are designed to handle. California residents need parallel preparedness for both sudden-onset earthquakes and rapid-evacuation wildfires, which have different gear priorities and timing dynamics.

The Pacific Northwest

The Pacific Northwest carries a threat that receives far less public attention than it deserves: the Cascadia Subduction Zone. When this offshore fault ruptures, and geologists are clear that it is a matter of when, not if, it will produce a magnitude 8 to 9 earthquake followed by a tsunami affecting the entire coastal zone from northern California through British Columbia. Coastal communities in Oregon and Washington have between fifteen and thirty minutes between shaking and wave arrival, depending on location. That is not a planning detail, it is a survival timeline.

If you live or work in a coastal Cascadia zone, your first response to a major earthquake is to move to high ground immediately, on foot if necessary, without waiting for an official warning. The warning may not come in time. Tsunami evacuation routes are marked in most coastal Oregon and Washington communities. Know yours before you need it, and walk it, because a route that takes ten minutes to drive can take twenty-five minutes on foot through a crowd.

Inland Pacific Northwest residents face different but still serious risks. Volcanic hazards from Mount Rainier, Mount Hood, and other Cascade peaks affect large populated areas. Lahar, the volcanic mudflow that would follow a major eruption or flank collapse on Rainier, could reach suburban Tacoma and Puyallup with little warning. Extended wet and cold weather after any regional disaster makes hypothermia risk higher than in most other regions. A Northwest emergency kit needs cold and wet weather capability year-round, not just in winter months.

Tornado Alley and the Central Plains

Tornadoes present a unique preparedness challenge because they are geographically precise in a way that other disasters are not. A tornado can destroy one house and leave the house next door untouched. This precision means that shelter selection matters more than supply quantity in tornado preparedness. The strongest shelter available within the time you have is the correct answer to a tornado warning, and that requires knowing before the warning what your options are.

Basements are the gold standard for tornado shelter and are common in the central plains in a way they are not in Florida or California. If you have one, know exactly where in the basement provides the most structural protection, typically under a staircase or in an interior room away from windows. If you don't have a basement, identify the lowest floor interior room with the most walls between you and the outside. Practice getting there quickly because tornado warnings give minutes, not hours.

Tornado Alley preparedness requires a different kit structure than most regional threats because the emergency is often very localized and very short. You may shelter in place for twenty minutes and then emerge to find your neighborhood destroyed while the town two miles away is completely unaffected. The recovery phase begins immediately, which means chainsaw access, heavy work gloves, and tools for debris removal become relevant within hours of the event. This is less true for hurricanes or earthquakes, where the disaster area is broad enough that recovery resources take days to arrive.

The warning system in tornado country is well-developed and worth understanding thoroughly. Tornado watches mean conditions are favorable for tornado development. Tornado warnings mean a tornado has been detected. The difference matters because a watch is a preparation signal and a warning is a take-shelter-immediately signal. Many central plains residents have a weather radio permanently mounted in their homes tuned to NOAA broadcasts. This is not cautious behavior in tornado country, it is basic infrastructure.

The Desert Southwest

The desert Southwest kills people through heat and dehydration with a speed that residents from temperate climates consistently underestimate. When I was hiking regularly in Joshua Tree and the Mojave, I watched park rangers deal with unprepared hikers several times who had run out of water in conditions that were genuinely life-threatening within a few hours. The desert doesn't give you time to improvise.

Water storage for desert emergency kits should be double what you think you need, and then add more. The calculation shifts entirely in extreme heat. At 110 degrees with physical exertion, a person can need a liter of water per hour. A 72-hour desert emergency at that consumption rate requires water quantities that most standard kits cannot carry. Desert residents need larger home water caches, vehicle water caches, and a clear understanding of where natural water sources exist along their likely evacuation routes.

Flash flooding is the desert hazard that kills people who think they understand desert risk. A thunderstorm twenty miles away in mountains you cannot see can send a wall of water down a dry wash with no warning. Never camp in or shelter in a wash or arroyo regardless of how dry the weather appears. Know the terrain around your location well enough to recognize drainage channels and get above them quickly if you hear thunder anywhere in the region.

Vehicle emergency kits in the desert Southwest need specific additions: a full-size spare tire and the knowledge and tools to change it, extra coolant and motor oil, a tow strap, jumper cables or a jump-start battery pack, and enough water for everyone in the vehicle for at least 24 hours beyond your planned trip. A breakdown on a desert highway in summer heat that keeps everyone in a car for several hours without water is a survival situation. It has killed people. Treating your vehicle like a survival system rather than just transportation is the correct desert mindset.

Mountain and High-Altitude Regions

Mountain emergencies have a characteristic that separates them from most other regional risks: isolation. During winter trips in the Sierra Nevada, I learned that a storm can cut a mountain community off from outside assistance for days. The roads close, the power goes out, and the nearest help is on the other side of a pass that is now impassable. Self-sufficiency requirements in mountain areas are not 72 hours, they are closer to a week in serious winter weather.

Altitude affects physiology in ways that compound every other emergency. Physical exertion at 8,000 feet requires significantly more effort than at sea level, dehydration happens faster because of lower humidity and increased breathing rate, and cold injuries develop more quickly because the thinner air reduces insulating capacity. A bug out bag that would sustain you for 72 hours at sea level may last 48 hours at altitude because you are consuming water and food faster and your body is working harder to stay warm.

Avalanche awareness is a specific mountain competency that no amount of general emergency preparedness replaces. If you live in or regularly travel through avalanche terrain, take an avalanche safety course, carry an avalanche beacon, probe, and shovel, and understand how to read terrain for avalanche risk. These are not casual additions to a bug out bag, they are a specialized safety system that requires training to use effectively. The beacon is worthless without the training to use it and companions who also have beacons and training. The gear itself is simple: a beacon runs $250–400, a collapsible probe and shovel together add another $100–150, and all three pack into a dedicated avalanche pack or strap to the outside of your bag. The investment is modest. The training is what most people skip, and skipping it makes the gear useless.

Urban and Dense Metropolitan Areas

Dense urban preparedness is genuinely different from suburban or rural preparedness, and most emergency guides are written with a garage, a car, and a backyard in mind. If you live in a high-rise apartment in Manhattan, Chicago, or San Francisco, those assumptions don't apply and the standard advice breaks down quickly.

Storage is the first problem. A full 72-hour kit for two people takes up significant volume, and a studio apartment may not have room for it. Urban preparedness requires more ruthless prioritization and compression than suburban preparedness. Focus on items that perform multiple functions, eliminate redundancies that rural residents can afford, and store supplies vertically and creatively. Under-bed storage, closet organizers, and furniture with storage built in all help. Accepting that your urban kit will be smaller and lighter than ideal is more useful than paralysis over not being able to build the perfect kit.

Evacuation from a high-rise building during a power outage means stairs, not elevators. A fully loaded pack that you can carry comfortably for a mile on flat ground becomes a serious problem when you are descending twenty flights of stairs. Urban residents in high floors should test their loaded bag on stairs before they need to do it under emergency conditions. Many people discover during this test that they need to reduce weight or redistribute the load.

Car-free urban residents need foot-based evacuation planning as a primary strategy rather than a backup. This means knowing your evacuation routes on foot, understanding which bridges and tunnels are likely to be closed versus open under different emergency types, and having destinations that are reachable without a vehicle. It also means your bug out bag must truly work as a carry system for several miles, not just a short walk to a parking garage. For car-free residents, the bag itself needs to be lighter and more carry-optimized than the standard build described in Chapter 1, because you have no fallback if it becomes too heavy to move. Aim for the lower end of the weight range. Your water strategy also shifts. You can't throw extra jugs in a trunk, so your purification redundancy matters more than stored volume. Know the location of your nearest designated emergency water distribution site before you need it, because that's your resupply point.

Urban water and sanitation problems after disasters are more acute than rural ones because the population density overwhelms public systems faster. After a major urban earthquake, broken water mains can leave millions of people without water simultaneously. Knowing where emergency water distribution points are likely to be established, and having enough stored water to reach them, is part of urban emergency planning that rural residents don't need to think about.

The Northeast and Mid-Atlantic

The Northeast threat profile is primarily winter weather, coastal storm surge from nor'easters and occasional hurricanes, and the specific vulnerability of aging urban infrastructure. Hurricane Sandy demonstrated in 2012 that coastal flooding can penetrate far inland through river systems and low-lying areas that residents assumed were safe, submerging subway systems, knocking out power for weeks, and cutting off barrier island communities entirely.

Winter preparedness in the Northeast means planning for extended power outages in cold weather, which is a different and more serious problem than a summer outage. A house without heat in January in Massachusetts or upstate New York loses temperature fast enough to become dangerous within 24 to 48 hours in severe cold. Emergency heating options, knowledge of which pipes to drain or protect, and a destination with heat for extended cold weather outages belong in every Northeast emergency plan. The generator rules from Chapter 15 are especially important in this context because people running generators indoors during cold weather to stay warm are among the most common carbon monoxide deaths in the country.

Adapting This Guide to Your Region

The regions above cover most of the country, but the principle extends to wherever you are. Identify your two or three most likely emergency scenarios based on actual local risk history, not general national statistics. Research your specific county or municipality's emergency plans, because local emergency management agencies publish threat assessments that are more useful than anything a national guide can offer for your specific location. Then use those scenarios to pressure-test the kit described in this book, and adjust what doesn't fit your reality.

Accessibility Needs

People with disabilities, chronic illnesses, or mobility limitations need considerations in emergency planning that go far beyond standard bug out bag preparations. I learned about accessibility needs during my disaster recovery work when we had to accommodate employees with various disabilities and medical conditions in our emergency plans.

Mobility limitations affect everything from bag selection to evacuation routes to shelter requirements. Someone who uses a wheelchair or walker can't carry a traditional backpack and can't evacuate on foot over rough terrain. During the Northridge earthquake, I saw people with mobility devices who couldn't navigate damaged sidewalks and debris-covered streets.

Wheelchair considerations require different approaches to emergency supplies and evacuation planning. Supplies might need to be attached to the wheelchair or carried by others. Evacuation routes need to be wheelchair accessible, eliminating many options that able-bodied people take for granted. During disasters, elevators don't work and many buildings become inaccessible to wheelchairs.

Medical equipment dependencies create additional challenges for people who rely on oxygen concentrators, dialysis machines, or other powered medical devices. During power outages, this equipment stops working, creating immediate life-threatening situations. Battery backups and backup power sources become essential, not just convenient.

I learned about medical equipment challenges during a regional power outage when a neighbor who used a home oxygen concentrator had to be evacuated to a hospital because his backup batteries couldn't power the device for an extended period. Having backup power sources and knowing where to get emergency medical care becomes critical for people with equipment dependencies.

Communication barriers affect people who are deaf, blind, or have other sensory impairments. Standard emergency alert systems might not work for people who can't hear sirens or see visual warnings. Alternative communication methods and assistance from others become necessary for receiving critical emergency information.

Service animal considerations add another layer of complexity to emergency planning. Service animals can't be separated from their handlers, but they also need food, water, and care during emergencies. Service animals might become stressed or disoriented during disasters, affecting their ability to provide assistance when it's needed most.

Cognitive and developmental disabilities create challenges related to understanding emergency situations and following complex instructions. People with these conditions might not understand why normal routines are being disrupted or why they need to leave familiar environments. Simple, clear instructions and familiar caregivers become important for managing these situations.

Medication management becomes more complex for people who take multiple medications or who have cognitive impairments that affect their ability to manage their own medications. During emergencies, medication schedules might be disrupted, pharmacies might be closed, and caregivers might not be available to provide assistance.

Support network coordination becomes essential for people who depend on others for daily assistance. During disasters, regular caregivers might not be available, transportation might not work, and communication systems might be down. Having backup plans and multiple support people becomes critical for maintaining necessary care.

Family caregiver considerations recognize that people who care for family members with disabilities or chronic conditions have additional responsibilities during emergencies. They need to plan for their own needs while also ensuring that the people they care for have adequate supplies and support. This often means larger emergency supply requirements and more complex evacuation planning.

Chapter 11: Maintenance and Testing

Regular Inventory Checks

A bug out bag that sits untouched for months or years is likely to fail you when you need it most. I learned this during a camping trip when I discovered that half the gear I thought I could depend on had deteriorated, expired, or simply stopped working. The batteries in my flashlight had leaked and corroded the contacts. The energy bars had turned into rock-hard blocks. Even the zipper on my sleeping bag had seized up from lack of use.

Emergency preparedness isn't a "set it and forget it" proposition. Your bug out bag is a dynamic system that requires regular attention to remain functional. Think of it like maintaining a car. You wouldn't expect your vehicle to run properly if you never changed the oil, checked the tires, or replaced worn parts. Your emergency gear needs the same kind of ongoing maintenance to be reliable when you need it.

I schedule formal inventory checks every six months, usually when daylight saving time changes. This timing works well because it's easy to remember and coincides with other household maintenance tasks like changing smoke detector batteries. During these checks, I remove everything from my bug out bag and examine each item individually.

Physical condition assessment is the first step in any inventory check. Look for signs of wear, damage, or deterioration that could affect functionality. Fabric items might show fraying, tears, or stains. Metal items could have rust or corrosion. Plastic items might crack or become brittle with age. I once discovered that a plastic water bottle had developed hairline cracks that would have leaked if I'd tried to use it.

Battery testing takes priority during inventory checks because battery failure is one of the most common equipment problems during emergencies. Even batteries that haven't been used can lose charge sitting on the shelf, and some types are prone to leaking corrosive chemicals that can destroy the devices they're meant to power. I test every battery-powered device and replace any batteries that show signs of weakness.

Expiration date verification affects more items than most people realize. Food and medications have obvious expiration dates, but water purification tablets, medications, sunscreen, and even some batteries also have limited shelf lives. I keep a written inventory with purchase dates and expiration dates for items that aren't clearly marked, because trying to remember when you bought something months later is nearly impossible.

Packaging integrity matters as much as the contents. Sealed packages that have been punctured can allow moisture, insects, or contamination to spoil the contents. Vacuum-sealed foods that have lost their seal might be unsafe to eat. Even small holes in packages can allow moisture to ruin items that should last for years. During one inventory check, I found that mice had chewed through several packages, contaminating the contents even though they hadn't eaten much.

Functionality testing means checking that gear works as intended, not just that it looks okay. Zippers can stick, snaps can break, and mechanical devices can fail even when they look fine. I test every zipper, buckle, snap, and moving part during inventory checks. Electronic devices get powered on and tested to ensure they still function properly.

Documentation updates become necessary as your life circumstances change. Contact information becomes outdated, insurance policies change, and medical conditions develop or resolve. Financial account information changes when you switch banks or get new credit cards. Emergency contact lists need updates when people move or change phone numbers.

Item Rotation Schedules

Different items in your bug out bag have different rotation requirements based on their shelf life, degradation rate, and importance to your survival. Understanding these different schedules helps you maintain freshness without wasting money on unnecessary replacements. I learned to create rotation schedules during my computer industry days when we had to manage equipment lifecycles and replacement cycles for critical systems.

Food rotation follows the "first in, first out" principle that grocery stores use to manage perishable inventory. Instead of just replacing expired items, I incorporate emergency food into my regular meals before it expires and replace it with fresh supplies. This approach ensures that my emergency food never gets stale and gives me practice eating the foods I might need to rely on during an emergency.

Water rotation schedules depend on your storage method and local conditions. Commercially bottled water has expiration dates, but the water itself doesn't really expire. The problem is that plastic bottles can degrade and develop off flavors, or they can be contaminated if they're stored in hot conditions. I replace stored water every year, using the old water for garden irrigation or household cleaning.

Battery replacement schedules vary dramatically by battery type and storage conditions. Alkaline batteries stored in cool, dry conditions can last for years, but batteries stored in hot garages or humid basements deteriorate much faster. I replace all batteries in my emergency kit annually, regardless of their rated shelf life, because battery failure during an emergency is too serious a risk to take chances with.

Chemical products like water purification tablets, medications, and even some adhesives have limited shelf lives that aren't always obvious. These items often degrade gradually, becoming less effective instead of completely useless. I replace chemical products every two years unless they have shorter expiration dates, because their effectiveness might be compromised even if they're not technically expired.

Fabric and textile rotation becomes necessary when items are exposed to moisture, temperature extremes, or UV light. Cotton clothing can develop mildew, synthetic fabrics can degrade from heat exposure, and elastic items like bungee cords lose their stretch. I inspect textile items carefully during inventory checks and replace anything that shows signs of deterioration.

Seasonal rotation acknowledges that your emergency needs change based on the time of year. Winter clothing that's essential in December is just dead weight in July. Cooling supplies that are critical during summer heat waves are useless during winter storms. I adjust my bug out bag contents seasonally, swapping out items that aren't appropriate for current conditions.

Gradual replacement spreads the cost of maintaining emergency supplies instead of requiring large expenditures all at once. I replace about one-third of my emergency supplies each year, cycling through different categories. This year I might focus on food and water, next year on clothing and equipment, and the following year on electronics and tools.

Practice Scenarios

Theoretical knowledge about emergency preparedness is useless if you can't apply it under stress. I learned this during my first CERT training exercise when I discovered that things I thought I understood completely became confusing and difficult when I was dealing with simulated emergency conditions. Reading about emergency procedures and performing them under pressure are completely different experiences.

Evacuation drills help you identify problems with your plans before you need to implement them during a real emergency. Time yourself packing your bug out bag and getting out of your house. Try doing it in the dark to simulate power outages. Practice evacuating from different parts of your house in case your primary exit is blocked. During my practice evacuations, I discovered that some of my gear was stored in places that would be difficult to reach quickly.

Equipment testing under realistic conditions reveals problems that don't show up during casual inspection. Set up your emergency shelter in your backyard during different weather conditions. Cook a meal using only your emergency cooking gear. Try to purify water using your emergency water treatment supplies. I learned about equipment limitations during a practice camping trip where my emergency stove wouldn't work properly in windy conditions.

Navigation practice helps you develop skills that GPS devices can't replace. Practice using a map and compass to find your way around your neighborhood. Learn to identify landmarks and judge distances. Try navigating at night using only a flashlight. During one practice session, I discovered that streets I drove every day looked completely different when I was walking at night during a power outage.

Communication exercises test your ability to contact family members and emergency services when normal methods might not work. Practice using two-way radios with family members. Test your emergency contact procedures when cell phone networks are congested. Learn to use alternative communication methods like social media check-in features. During Hurricane Sandy, some of my relatives discovered that text messages got through when voice calls wouldn't.

Stress simulation acknowledges that emergency situations create physical and psychological stress that affects your ability to think clearly and perform tasks. Practice emergency procedures when you're tired, cold, hungry, or dealing with time pressure. The skills you can perform easily under ideal conditions might become much more difficult when you're stressed and uncomfortable.

Family coordination exercises become critical if your emergency plans involve multiple family members. Practice your communication plans, meeting procedures, and coordination protocols. Different family members might need to take responsibility for different aspects of emergency response, and everyone needs to understand their role. During family practice sessions, we discovered that our young children had completely different ideas about what they were supposed to do during an emergency. That lesson stuck, and even adults who think they understand the plan often find gaps when they actually run through it.

Problem-solving scenarios help you develop the mental flexibility to adapt when things don't go according to plan. Practice dealing with equipment failures, blocked routes, and unexpected complications. What would you do if your primary evacuation route was impassable? How would you handle it if critical equipment failed? These scenarios help you think through alternatives before you need them.

Skill Development

Physical preparedness often gets overlooked in favor of equipment and supplies, but your body is the most important tool you have during an emergency. I learned this during that Christmas hike when my father and I got trapped in the canyon. My lack of physical conditioning made the emergency much more difficult than it needed to be. Climbing out of that canyon was exhausting work that would have been much easier if I'd been in better shape.

Cardiovascular fitness affects your ability to handle the physical demands of emergency situations. Evacuating on foot with a heavy pack, walking long distances to reach safety, or performing physical work during disaster recovery all require basic cardiovascular conditioning. You don't need to be an athlete, but you should be able to walk several miles carrying a reasonable load without becoming exhausted.

Strength training helps with carrying emergency gear and performing tasks like moving debris, setting up shelters, or helping injured people. Upper body strength becomes important for carrying packs and lifting objects. Core strength helps with balance and stability when walking on uneven terrain or carrying unbalanced loads. I started doing basic strength training after realizing how difficult it was to carry a fully loaded bug out bag for any distance.

Basic first aid skills can mean the difference between life and death when professional medical help isn't available. Learn to control bleeding, treat burns, stabilize fractures, and recognize signs of serious medical conditions. Practice these skills regularly because medical procedures that seem simple in theory can be difficult to perform on real people who are injured and in pain.

I took a wilderness first aid course after my mountain hiking experiences, and it completely changed my perspective on medical preparedness. The course included hands-on practice with realistic injury scenarios, and I discovered that treating injuries in field conditions is much more challenging than treating them in a clean, well-lit classroom setting.

Fire starting skills become critical when you need warmth, light, or the ability to cook food and purify water. Practice starting fires in different weather conditions using various methods and materials. Learn to build fires that burn efficiently and safely. During winter camping trips, I practiced fire starting in wet and windy conditions until I could reliably get a fire going even when conditions were difficult.

Knot tying knowledge helps you use rope and cordage effectively for securing gear, creating shelters, and handling equipment. Learn a few basic knots that can handle most situations: bowline for creating loops, clove hitch for securing lines to objects, and trucker's hitch for creating mechanical advantage when tightening lines. Practice tying these knots until you can do them quickly and in the dark.

Tool usage skills ensure you can use the equipment in your bug out bag effectively. Practice using your multi-tool, knife, and other equipment for various tasks. Learn to maintain and sharpen your tools so they remain functional. During one practice session, I realized that I'd been using my multi-tool incorrectly for certain tasks, making jobs much harder than they needed to be.

Mental preparedness involves developing the psychological resilience to handle emergency situations without panicking or making poor decisions. Practice staying calm under pressure. Learn stress management techniques that work for you. Develop the mental flexibility to adapt when plans change or equipment fails. Emergency situations test your mental stamina as much as your physical capabilities.

Walk through emergency scenarios in your head the same way a pilot runs through a checklist before takeoff: not because you expect the landing gear to fail, but because when something does go wrong, the sequence is already in your muscle memory. I've run the earthquake scenario in my head enough times that the first three minutes are automatic. That automatic response is exactly what you're building when you practice.

Chapter 12: Multiple Bug Out Bag Strategy

Individual vs. Family Systems

The question of how many bug out bags you need doesn't have a simple answer, and it took me years of trial and error to figure out the right approach when I was planning for a family. My first mistake was thinking that one complete bag would handle all situations for everyone. I learned during family camping trips that this approach fails miserably when you have multiple people with different needs, capabilities, and responsibilities.

Individual carry bags make sense for anyone old enough and strong enough to carry their own equipment. During the Northridge earthquake, we had to walk several miles through debris-covered streets, and having everyone carry part of the load would have been much more manageable than one person struggling with an oversized pack. Even children can carry age-appropriate emergency supplies in small backpacks that they're familiar with using.

I learned about individual responsibility during a CERT training exercise where families had to evacuate together. The families where everyone had their own emergency kit moved faster and more efficiently than families trying to manage one large bag. When people are responsible for their own supplies, they're more likely to know what they have and how to use it.

Personal bag sizing depends on the person's age, strength, and hiking experience. A fit adult might be able to carry 25-30 pounds for several miles, but someone who's out of shape or dealing with mobility issues might struggle with even 15 pounds. Children's bags should focus on lightweight essentials: water, snacks, comfort items, and maybe a small flashlight. The goal is making them feel involved and responsible without overloading them.

Contents allow each family member's bag to reflect their individual needs and capabilities. When my family was together, my wife's bag included different medications and feminine hygiene supplies. My teenage son's bag had more food because he ate constantly. My daughter's bag included her inhaler and extra batteries for her hearing aids. Customizing bags for individual needs makes more sense than trying to create one-size-fits-all solutions.

Coordination challenges arise when you have multiple individual bags instead of one centralized system. Who carries the water purification tablets? Where are the emergency tools stored? How do you avoid duplication of heavy items like first aid supplies? I learned to designate one person as the "pack leader" who carries shared equipment while everyone else focuses on personal supplies.

Load distribution becomes critical when you have multiple people carrying gear. Heavy shared items like tools, cooking equipment, and shelter materials get distributed among the strongest carriers. Essential items like water and food get divided so that losing one person's pack doesn't leave the whole family without critical supplies. Everyone should know what everyone else is carrying in case redistribution becomes necessary.

Vehicle-Based Bags

Car emergency kits serve different purposes than personal carry bags and can include larger, heavier items that would be impractical to carry on foot. During the forest fire evacuation that trapped me on the mountain road, I realized that having supplies in my vehicle could have made a huge difference in my ability to wait out the emergency or even self-rescue if necessary.

Vehicle bags can be much larger and heavier than personal carry bags because you're not limited by what you can carry on your back. I keep a large duffle bag in my car with supplies that would be impossible to include in a walking bag: extra water, more extensive first aid supplies, additional tools, and even a small tent. The trade-off is that these supplies are only useful if you have access to your vehicle.

Climate considerations become important for vehicle-stored supplies because cars experience much more extreme temperatures than indoor storage. Medications can degrade in hot cars, batteries can freeze in cold weather, and food items can spoil faster in temperature extremes. I learned to choose vehicle emergency supplies that can handle temperature swings and to rotate temperature-sensitive items more frequently.

Multi-purpose items make sense for vehicle kits where space is less constrained than weight. A larger first aid kit with more complete supplies. A full-sized multi-tool instead of a compact one. Multiple methods for starting fires. Vehicle kits can include backup options that personal bags can't accommodate.

Accessibility planning ensures you can reach your vehicle emergency supplies even if your car is damaged or stuck. During the earthquake, some people couldn't get into their cars because garage doors wouldn't open or vehicles were blocked by debris. I keep my vehicle emergency kit in the passenger compartment instead of the trunk so I can access it even if the car is damaged.

Seasonal adjustments for vehicle kits should be more complete than personal bag adjustments because you have more space to work with. Complete winter emergency gear: extra blankets, warm clothing, and heating supplies. Summer gear with additional water, cooling supplies, and sun protection. Vehicle kits can accommodate seasonal equipment that personal bags can't carry.

Security considerations matter for vehicle-stored emergency supplies because cars are easier to break into than homes. Valuable items stored in vehicles can attract thieves, and medical supplies might be attractive to drug users. I avoid storing cash, expensive equipment, or controlled substances in my vehicle emergency kit, keeping those items in my personal carry bag or home storage.

Workplace Preparations

Office emergency kits address the reality that many people spend more waking hours at work than at home, making workplace preparedness just as important as home preparedness. During the Northridge earthquake, many people were at home. But earthquakes, fires, and other emergencies can happen during business hours when you're away from your home emergency supplies.

Workplace emergency supplies need to be appropriate for office environments where storing large amounts of gear might not be practical or acceptable. A small kit that fits in a desk drawer might be all you can manage in some offices. I keep basic supplies at work: water, energy bars, a small first aid kit, a flashlight, and copies of important documents. Nothing that would raise eyebrows but enough to handle basic emergency needs.

Building considerations affect what supplies make sense for workplace kits. High-rise buildings present different challenges than ground-floor offices. Urban offices have different resource availability than rural workplaces. Some buildings have complete emergency procedures and supplies, while others leave emergency preparedness entirely up to individual employees.

I learned about building needs during emergency drills at various workplaces. Some buildings had excellent emergency procedures and well-stocked supply caches. Others had barely functional emergency lighting and no emergency supplies at all. Understanding your building's emergency capabilities helps you determine what personal supplies you need to keep at work.

Evacuation procedures at work might be completely different from home evacuation plans. You might need to evacuate to assembly areas, follow designated routes, or wait for instructions from building management. Workplace emergency supplies should support these procedures instead of conflicting with them. Knowing your building's emergency procedures is just as important as having supplies.

Coworker coordination can enhance everyone's emergency preparedness without requiring large individual investments. A group of coworkers might coordinate their workplace emergency supplies to avoid duplication and ensure complete coverage. One person might focus on first aid supplies, another on communication equipment, and a third on food and water.

Legal and policy considerations might limit what emergency supplies you can keep at work. Some workplaces prohibit knives, medications, or other items that would normally be part of emergency kits. Understanding your workplace policies helps you plan appropriate emergency supplies that won't violate company rules or get you in trouble with security.

Transportation backup planning recognizes that getting home from work during an emergency might not be possible. Public transportation might be shut down, roads might be blocked, and personal vehicles might be inaccessible. Workplace emergency supplies should include items that would help you shelter in place at work or walk home if necessary.

Home Storage Systems

Home emergency supplies serve as your primary cache and command center for emergency preparedness. Unlike portable bags that are limited by weight and space constraints, home storage can include larger quantities of supplies, backup equipment, and items that support longer-term emergencies. During the extended power outages after the ice storm, having complete home emergency supplies made the difference between mild inconvenience and serious hardship.

Centralized storage in a dedicated location makes inventory management easier and ensures that supplies are accessible when needed. I converted a closet into an emergency supply center where everything is organized and readily accessible. Having supplies scattered throughout the house means you might not be able to find what you need quickly during a crisis.

Distributed backup storage provides redundancy in case your primary storage area becomes inaccessible. Small caches of critical supplies stored in different areas of your home ensure that you can access emergency supplies even if part of your house is damaged or blocked. I keep backup supplies in the garage, basement, and even a small cache in an outside storage shed.

Scale considerations for home storage allow you to prepare for longer emergencies than portable bags can handle. Instead of three days' worth of supplies, home storage can support weeks or even months of self-sufficiency. Larger water storage, more extensive food supplies, additional tools, and backup equipment that wouldn't fit in portable bags.

Climate control becomes important for home emergency storage because many homes experience temperature and humidity fluctuations that can damage supplies. Basements might flood, attics get extremely hot, and garages experience temperature swings that can ruin food, medications, and equipment. I learned to choose storage locations based on environmental stability, not just convenience.

Access planning ensures that home emergency supplies remain available even if normal access routes are blocked. During the earthquake, some people couldn't get to their emergency supplies because doorways were jammed or rooms were blocked by debris. I store emergency supplies in multiple locations and ensure that at least one cache can be accessed from outside the house.

Integration with portable systems means that home storage supports and resupplies your portable emergency bags instead of duplicating them. Home storage can include bulk supplies that you use to restock portable bags, seasonal equipment that gets swapped in and out of portable bags, and backup gear that replaces portable equipment when it wears out or gets lost.

Inventory management for home storage requires more systems than portable bag management because you're dealing with larger quantities and more diverse supplies. I maintain written inventories with expiration dates, rotation schedules, and usage tracking. Home storage supplies need regular attention to prevent spoilage and ensure that supplies remain fresh and functional.

Security considerations for home emergency storage recognize that large stockpiles of supplies might attract unwanted attention during emergencies. Keeping home emergency supplies discrete and secure helps prevent theft while ensuring that they're available when your family needs them. I avoid discussing my emergency supplies with people who don't need to know, and I store valuable supplies in secure locations within my home.

Chapter 13: When Minutes Matter

The Reality of Emergency Timing

Emergency preparedness planning often assumes you'll have reasonable warning before you need to evacuate, but real disasters don't follow polite schedules or give you time to pack thoughtfully. My friend Sabrina learned this during the massive San Diego fires when she had exactly two minutes to grab what she could and get out. Two minutes. Not enough time to think, barely enough time to act on pure instinct and whatever preparations she'd made in advance.

During the Lake Arrowhead fires, people who had lived through decades of fire seasons and thought they understood wildfire behavior suddenly found themselves with less than an hour's warning before mandatory evacuations. These weren't people caught off guard by their first emergency. These were mountain residents who'd seen fires before, who thought they knew how fast things could change. The fire moved faster than anyone expected, and the evacuation window slammed shut with terrifying speed.

The Northridge earthquake gave us a different kind of brutal timing lesson. The shaking stopped at 4:31 AM, and within a couple of hours, authorities were ordering evacuations from damaged buildings and areas with gas leaks. People who'd been jolted awake by the earthquake found themselves having to make life-or-death decisions about what to take and what to leave behind while they were still disoriented and trying to assess what had just happened.

These timing realities destroy most people's emergency plans because those plans assume you'll have time to think, time to gather supplies, time to make careful decisions about what to take. When you have minutes or even seconds to react, all that careful planning becomes useless unless you've prepared for speed.

I learned about timing pressure during a CERT training exercise where they simulated a building collapse with toxic gas leaks. We had three minutes to evacuate and secure our area. Three minutes sounds like plenty of time until you're dealing with injured people, blocked exits, and equipment that doesn't work the way you expected. People who seemed calm and competent during classroom training became flustered and made poor decisions when the clock was ticking.

The psychological effects of time pressure can't be underestimated. When you're told you have minutes to evacuate, your brain doesn't work normally. You forget obvious things, you make irrational decisions about what's important, and you waste precious seconds on items that don't matter while leaving behind things that could save your life. Adrenaline helps with physical performance but hurts decision-making ability.

Physical limitations become magnified under time pressure. Tasks that normally take a few minutes suddenly take much longer when you're stressed and hurried. Simple things like finding keys, locking doors, or loading a car become frustratingly difficult when every second counts and your hands are shaking from adrenaline.

Zero-Notice Scenarios

Some emergencies give you no warning at all. Earthquakes strike without any advance notice. Flash floods can go from clear skies to life-threatening water in minutes. Building collapses, explosions, and other sudden disasters leave you with whatever you have immediately available or can grab within arm's reach.

Earthquake preparedness has to assume you'll go from sound sleep to full emergency in seconds. During the Northridge earthquake, we went from peaceful sleep to complete chaos in the time it took the building to start shaking. There was no time to gather supplies, no time to make plans, no time to do anything except react to immediate threats and try to stay alive.

The supplies that mattered during those first critical minutes weren't the carefully organized emergency kits stored in closets. They were the flashlight next to the bed, the shoes under the nightstand that protected our feet from broken glass, and the emergency radio that we could grab while stumbling through the dark apartment. Everything else was worthless because we couldn't get to it safely.

Immediate access becomes the only thing that matters during zero-notice emergencies. If you can't reach it in the dark, while the ground is shaking, while debris is falling, then it might as well not exist. This reality forced me to completely rethink where I store emergency supplies and what I keep within arm's reach of my bed.

Sleep considerations become critical because many emergencies happen at night when you're most vulnerable. You're disoriented, your night vision is poor, you're not fully dressed, and you don't have immediate access to most of your gear. I learned to keep a small emergency kit next to my bed with the bare essentials: flashlight, shoes, keys, and enough supplies to get me safely out of the building.

Vehicle access during zero-notice emergencies often isn't possible because garage doors won't open without power, cars might be blocked by debris, or the vehicles themselves might be damaged. During the earthquake, many people couldn't get to their cars for hours because garage doors were stuck and debris blocked driveways. Emergency plans that depend on vehicle access can fail completely during sudden-onset disasters.

Clothing considerations matter because zero-notice emergencies might catch you in pajamas or unprepared for current weather conditions. I keep clothes and shoes next to my bed that would be appropriate for current weather and allow me to function outside my house. Being forced to evacuate in bare feet and nightclothes turns a manageable emergency into a potential disaster.

Two-Minute Evacuations

Sabrina's experience during the San Diego fires represents one of the most challenging emergency scenarios: enough warning to know you need to evacuate but not enough time to gather supplies thoughtfully. Two minutes is barely enough time to grab your keys and get out the door, let alone pack supplies for an extended evacuation.

Pre-positioned supplies become essential for ultra-short evacuation windows. If your bug out bag isn't already packed and sitting by the door, you won't have time to gather supplies during a two-minute evacuation. Sabrina had maybe 30 seconds to grab essentials before she had to get in her car and drive away from the approaching fire. Everything else had to be left behind.

Priority decisions under extreme time pressure reveal what really matters versus what you think matters. When you have two minutes, you don't have time to save photo albums, important documents, or sentimental items. You have time to save lives and grab the one or two most critical items. Sabrina grabbed her purse and her cat. Everything else became a casualty of timing.

Sabrina didn't have time to think during her evacuation. She grabbed the things that were part of her daily routine: purse, keys, and the cat carrier she kept ready because she lived in fire country. Conscious decision-making had already left the building. What remained was habit. That's what two-minute evacuations run on.

Vehicle readiness takes on critical importance during short-notice evacuations. If your car doesn't start immediately, if you're low on gas, or if you have to clear items out of your car before you can use it, you might not make it out in time. Sabrina's car started on the first try and had enough gas to get her to safety, but she'd seen neighbors whose cars wouldn't start or who wasted precious minutes trying to load belongings into vehicles that weren't ready to go.

Communication challenges during rapid evacuations mean you might not have time to contact family members or coordinate with others. Cell phone networks often overload during mass evacuations, and you might not have time to wait for calls to go through. Sabrina couldn't reach her family members until hours after her evacuation because everyone was trying to use their phones at the same time.

Route planning becomes critical because main evacuation routes quickly become gridlocked during mass evacuations. Knowing alternate routes and being prepared to abandon your vehicle if necessary can mean the difference between escaping and being trapped. During Sabrina's evacuation, the main highway out of the area became completely blocked within minutes, and people who knew back roads were the only ones who made it out quickly.

One-Hour Warnings

An hour's notice feels like luxury compared to two-minute evacuations, but it's still not enough time for careful preparation if you haven't planned in advance. During the Lake Arrowhead evacuations, even residents who'd been through fire evacuations before found themselves scrambling to decide what to take and struggling to fit their choices into their vehicles.

Systematic approaches become possible with an hour's warning, but you still need to have systems ready to implement. You can't develop an evacuation plan during the evacuation itself. The people who succeeded during the Lake Arrowhead evacuations were those who'd already decided what they would take and had practiced their evacuation procedures.

Load prioritization becomes a real challenge when you have time to gather supplies but limited space to transport them. An hour gives you time to load your car thoughtfully, but you still have to make hard choices about what fits and what gets left behind. Having predetermined priorities and pre-positioned supplies makes these decisions easier when you're under stress.

I learned about one-hour evacuation challenges during a wildfire threat near my home several years ago. I had about 45 minutes' warning before I might need to evacuate. Even with my emergency preparedness background, I found myself struggling to decide what to take and second-guessing my choices. An hour sounds like plenty of time until you're doing it.

Family coordination becomes both possible and necessary with an hour's warning. You have time to make sure everyone knows what's happening and what they need to do, but you also have to spend time on coordination that you didn't need during shorter evacuations. Making sure everyone is ready to go at the same time can be challenging when family members are scattered or focusing on different tasks.

Last-minute additions often create problems during one-hour evacuations because people convince themselves they have time to grab additional items. The families who succeeded during Lake Arrowhead evacuations were those who stuck to their predetermined evacuation plans and resisted the temptation to add more items. The families who got in trouble were those who kept thinking of "one more thing" they should take.

Vehicle loading strategies become important when you have time to pack but need to do it efficiently. Random loading wastes space and can make your vehicle unsafe to drive. Having a planned approach to loading your vehicle saves time and ensures you can fit essential items safely.

Extended Warning Periods

Multi-hour warnings, like those sometimes available during hurricane evacuations, create different challenges because you have enough time to overthink your decisions and second-guess your plans. When the Northridge earthquake damaged buildings and infrastructure, some areas had several hours before mandatory evacuations were ordered, and people struggled with having too much time to think about what to take.

Decision paralysis becomes a real problem when you have hours to decide what to take and where to go. People who had managed two-minute evacuations effectively sometimes fell apart when they had time to consider all their options. The abundance of time led to overthinking that paralyzed decision-making instead of improving it.

Supply expansion happens when people convince themselves that having more time means they should take more supplies. Instead of sticking to proven emergency kits, people start adding items they wouldn't normally consider essential. This expansion often leads to overloaded vehicles, delayed departures, and supplies that aren't useful during evacuations.

False security can develop when warnings extend over many hours or days. People start to believe that having more time makes the evacuation less serious or that they might not need to evacuate at all. This false security can lead to delayed departures that put people in danger when conditions deteriorate faster than expected.

I experienced this during a wildfire watch that lasted for two days before we were ordered to evacuate. By the second day, the constant state of alert had worn down everyone's sense of urgency. When the evacuation order came, it took longer than it should have to shift from "maybe we'll need to leave" to "we need to leave right now."

Resource management becomes both an opportunity and a challenge during extended warnings. You have time to gather additional supplies, fuel vehicles, and prepare your home for evacuation, but you also risk exhausting yourself with preparation activities that might not be necessary. Balancing preparation with conservation of energy and resources requires discipline.

Departure timing decisions become critical when you have extended warning periods. Leaving too early might mean unnecessary disruption if the threat doesn't materialize. Leaving too late might mean getting caught in traffic jams or deteriorating conditions. The people who navigate this timing successfully are those who set criteria for departure and stick to them regardless of external pressure.

Building Time-Critical Skills

Preparation for rapid evacuations requires different skills and approaches than preparation for longer-term emergencies.

Speed becomes more important than completeness, and decision-making under pressure becomes more critical than complete planning. These skills need to be developed through practice because they don't come naturally to most people.

Speed packing techniques help you gather essential items quickly without forgetting critical supplies. This isn't the same as normal packing where you have time to think through everything you might need. Speed packing focuses on predetermined essentials and ignores everything else. I practice this by timing myself gathering my emergency supplies and trying to improve my speed without sacrificing critical items.

Memorization of critical locations helps you find essential items quickly when you're stressed and working in unfamiliar conditions like darkness or smoke. Knowing exactly where your keys, important documents, medications, and emergency supplies are located without having to think about it saves precious time during rapid evacuations.

Physical conditioning affects your ability to move quickly while carrying emergency supplies. If you can't move quickly with a loaded emergency bag, you might have to abandon supplies that could be critical for your survival after evacuation. Basic fitness isn't just about long-term health, it's about emergency capability.

Mental rehearsal of emergency scenarios helps you perform effectively when real emergencies happen. Visualizing evacuation scenarios, practicing decision-making under time pressure, and mentally rehearsing emergency procedures all help you respond more effectively when emergencies occur. Emergency situations aren't the time to figure out what you should do.

The fire on the mountain road gave me about ninety seconds from the moment I understood what was happening to the moment the firefighter appeared at my window. Those ninety seconds felt like nothing. If I had spent them panicking instead of thinking, the outcome would have been different. Controlled breathing, conscious focus, and some version of "okay, what are my options right now" are the difference between those two outcomes. Practice them when nothing is wrong so they show up when something is.

Chapter 14: Integration with Emergency Plans

Home Emergency Plans

Your bug out bag is just one piece of a larger emergency preparedness puzzle, and it needs to work together with your overall home emergency plan. I learned this during the Northridge earthquake when having emergency supplies was only part of what we needed. We also needed communication plans, evacuation routes, meeting places, and coordination with neighbors. The bug out bag that sits in isolation from these broader plans is like having a spare tire without a jack.

Family communication plans become critical when disasters scatter family members or disrupt normal contact methods. During the earthquake, our family was separated and we had no way to coordinate our response because we'd never established communication procedures. My bug out bag had emergency supplies, but it didn't help us find our missing son or let extended family know we were okay.

I learned to integrate communication planning with bug out bag preparations by keeping contact information for out-of-area relatives who could serve as communication hubs. Local phone networks often fail during disasters, but long-distance calls sometimes get through. Having predetermined contact persons and communication schedules means everyone knows how to reconnect even when normal methods don't work.

Meeting places need to be predetermined and known to all family members because disasters often prevent people from returning home. Primary meeting places should be close to home for minor emergencies. Secondary meeting places should be outside your immediate neighborhood for disasters that affect larger areas. Everyone should know both locations and how to get there from common places like work, school, or shopping areas.

Evacuation routes require more planning than most people realize because main roads often become impassable or gridlocked during mass evacuations. During the forest fire that trapped me on the mountain road, the primary evacuation route was completely blocked, and people who knew alternate routes were the only ones who escaped quickly. Your bug out bag is useless if you can't get out of the danger zone.

I practiced evacuation routes during non-emergency times, driving different routes at different times of day to understand how long they take and what obstacles might exist. Some routes that work fine during normal traffic become impossible during rush hour or when thousands of people are trying to evacuate simultaneously. Having multiple planned routes with different characteristics gives you options when conditions change.

Shelter planning addresses where you'll go if you can't return home for days or weeks. Hotels fill up quickly during major disasters, and emergency shelters have limitations on what supplies you can bring and how long you can stay. Having predetermined arrangements with friends or relatives in other areas provides alternatives when public shelters aren't available or appropriate.

Home preparation procedures help you secure your property before evacuating and can prevent additional damage while you're gone. Shutting off utilities, securing loose items that could become projectiles, and protecting important documents all take time that you might not have during rapid evacuations. Having predetermined procedures and practiced routines makes these tasks faster and more effective.

Neighbor coordination can multiply everyone's preparedness effectiveness without requiring large individual investments. During the earthquake, neighbors with medical training helped treat injuries, neighbors with tools helped clear debris, and neighbors with working radios provided information. Knowing your neighbors' skills and resources before emergencies happen creates an informal support network that benefits everyone.

Vehicle Emergency Kits

Your vehicle emergency kit serves a different purpose than your home bug out bag and needs to integrate with your evacuation and travel plans. During that forest fire evacuation, I realized that having supplies in my vehicle could have made the difference between a manageable delay and a life-threatening situation. Vehicle kits handle different scenarios than walking evacuation bags and need different contents and procedures.

Extended travel considerations recognize that evacuations often involve longer trips than normal daily driving. You might need to drive hundreds of miles to reach safe areas, and normal gas stations might be closed or have long lines. Vehicle emergency kits should include supplies for longer trips: extra food, water, medications, and tools for basic vehicle maintenance.

Vehicle breakdown scenarios become more serious during emergency evacuations when normal services aren't available. Tow trucks might not be operating, repair shops might be closed, and cell phone coverage might be spotty. Your vehicle emergency kit should include basic tools for minor repairs, supplies for signaling for help, and provisions for waiting extended periods for assistance.

I learned about vehicle breakdown preparedness during a camping trip when my car broke down in a remote area with no cell coverage. The basic tools and supplies I had in my vehicle emergency kit allowed me to make temporary repairs and signal for help. Without those supplies, a minor mechanical problem could have become a serious survival situation.

Climate control in vehicles becomes critical during extended delays or overnight stays in your car. Vehicles can become dangerously hot or cold depending on weather conditions, and you might need to spend hours or even overnight in your car during evacuations. Vehicle emergency kits should include supplies for temperature regulation that wouldn't be necessary in personal carry bags.

Fuel management requires planning beyond just keeping your tank full. During mass evacuations, gas stations quickly run out of fuel or lose power and can't pump gas. Knowing where alternative fuel sources are located and having backup transportation plans helps when your primary vehicle can't be refueled. Some people carry additional fuel containers, but this requires careful safety considerations.

Communication equipment in vehicles can include more powerful radios and better antennas than portable devices. Vehicle-mounted communication equipment can reach longer distances and provide more reliable contact with emergency services or family members. During widespread disasters, vehicle-based communication might be your only reliable contact with the outside world.

Vehicle loading procedures help you quickly transfer supplies from your home to your vehicle during evacuations. Having predetermined loading plans and practiced procedures means you can efficiently pack your vehicle without forgetting essential items or overloading it beyond safe capacity. Random loading wastes space and can make your vehicle unsafe to drive.

Workplace Preparedness

Workplace emergency preparedness requires different approaches than home preparedness because you have less control over your environment and might need to coordinate with building management or coworkers. During the earthquake, people who were at work faced different challenges than those who were at home, and many workplace emergency plans proved inadequate when tested by a real disaster.

Building emergency procedures vary dramatically between workplaces, and understanding your building's procedures is just as important as having personal emergency supplies. Some buildings have excellent emergency plans with designated wardens, regular drills, and complete supply caches. Others have minimal procedures and leave emergency preparedness entirely up to individual employees.

I learned about workplace preparedness variations during my career in different industries and buildings. High-rise buildings had sophisticated evacuation procedures but limited ability to shelter in place. Ground-floor buildings had easier evacuation but different security concerns. Industrial facilities had hazards that required different emergency procedures than office buildings.

Personal workspace supplies need to be appropriate for your work environment while still providing essential emergency capabilities. Large emergency kits might not be acceptable in open office environments, but small kits that fit in desk drawers can provide basic emergency supplies without creating workplace issues. The key is balancing preparedness needs with workplace constraints.

Coordination with coworkers can enhance everyone's emergency preparedness without requiring large individual investments. Groups of coworkers can coordinate their workplace emergency supplies to ensure complete coverage without duplication. One person might focus on first aid supplies, another on communication equipment, and a third on food and water supplies.

Transportation alternatives become critical when normal transportation systems fail during emergencies. Public transportation often shuts down during disasters, and personal vehicles might be inaccessible if parking structures are damaged or roads are blocked. Having plans for walking home from work or reaching alternate transportation points helps when normal travel isn't possible.

Communication with family becomes challenging when workplace communication systems are overloaded or damaged. Having predetermined communication plans that account for workplace limitations helps ensure you can contact family members and coordinate response plans even when you're separated by the emergency.

Professional responsibilities might conflict with personal emergency plans if your job involves emergency response or essential services. Healthcare workers, emergency responders, and utility workers often have obligations to remain at work during emergencies when others are evacuating. Balancing professional responsibilities with family safety requires careful planning and communication.

Community Resources

Community emergency resources can supplement your personal preparedness but shouldn't be the foundation of your emergency plans. During major disasters, community resources often become overwhelmed or unavailable, making personal preparedness even more important. Understanding what community resources exist and how to access them helps you make better decisions during emergencies.

Emergency shelters provide temporary housing when you can't return home or stay with friends and relatives. Understanding shelter locations, capacity, and rules helps you plan for scenarios where sheltering might be necessary. Most emergency shelters have strict rules about what supplies you can bring and how long you can stay, affecting how you plan your bug out bag contents.

I learned about emergency shelter realities during disaster response training where we toured shelter facilities. The conditions were basic but adequate for short-term stays. Shelters often reached capacity quickly during major disasters, and people who arrived late sometimes found no space available. Having shelter as a backup plan while maintaining other options proved most effective.

Medical facilities and their emergency procedures become important when family members need medical care during disasters. Hospitals often operate on backup power with limited capabilities, and normal medical offices might be closed or inaccessible. Knowing which medical facilities are most likely to remain operational helps you plan for medical emergencies during disasters.

Transportation resources during emergencies might include public evacuation buses, emergency transportation for people with disabilities, or coordination points for carpooling. Understanding what transportation assistance might be available helps you plan evacuation options for family members who can't drive or don't have vehicles available.

Food and water distribution points provide emergency supplies when personal supplies are exhausted or unavailable. These distribution points often take time to establish and might have long lines or limited supplies. Knowing where they're likely to be located helps with planning, but personal supplies remain more reliable than depending on public distribution.

Communication resources like emergency broadcast stations, public information hotlines, and community bulletin boards provide information about emergency conditions and recovery resources. Knowing how to access official information helps you make better decisions about when to evacuate, where to go, and when it's safe to return home.

Volunteer organizations often provide assistance during disasters but might take time to organize and deploy. Understanding what volunteer assistance might be available helps you plan for recovery activities, but immediate emergency response usually depends on personal preparedness and informal community support.

Government emergency services like police, fire, and emergency management operate under different procedures during major disasters. Response times might be much longer than normal, and services might be prioritized for life-threatening emergencies. Understanding how emergency services operate during disasters helps you set realistic expectations and plan accordingly.

Community preparedness networks (neighborhood emergency response teams, ham radio groups, volunteer fire departments) create relationships before disasters that pay off during them. The CERT training I did years ago is still the reason I know my neighbors' names, which exit routes exist in my building, and how the incident command system actually works. That knowledge came from showing up before anything was wrong.

Chapter 15: When Staying Put Is the Answer

Shelter in Place vs. Bugging Out

The framing of this book has been about getting out fast, and for good reason. But one of the most important decisions you'll face during an emergency isn't how to pack your bag, it's whether to pack it at all. Sometimes the safest thing you can do is stay exactly where you are.

During Hurricane Milton, I made the decision to shelter in place in my Florida apartment. I'd evaluated the storm track, checked the surge maps for my area, confirmed I wasn't in an evacuation zone, and concluded that riding it out was safer than joining the mass exodus that jams Florida's highways before every major storm. People have died in their cars trying to evacuate when they would have been perfectly safe staying home. That decision requires information, preparation, and the discipline to resist the pull toward action when staying still is the right call.

The decision framework is simple once you understand it. You shelter in place when the threat is better managed by staying inside your home than by traveling through it. You evacuate when remaining puts you in greater danger than leaving. The tricky part is that you often have to make this call before you know which way things will break.

Hazardous material incidents illustrate this clearly. If a train derails nearby and releases toxic chemicals, getting in your car and driving through the contaminated area is far more dangerous than sealing up your house and waiting for authorities to give the all-clear. Your home becomes a filter and a barrier. The same logic applies to certain industrial accidents, nuclear events, and situations where the roads themselves are the danger zone. Wildfire scenarios are almost always evacuate situations because fire moves faster than most people expect, as I've seen firsthand. But severe winter storms often favor sheltering in place because the roads become the danger. Civil unrest and active threat situations frequently call for staying put and locked down rather than exposing yourself to whatever is happening outside. Pandemics are a specific category of their own, where shelter in place becomes a long-term strategy measured in weeks rather than hours.

Home Hardening for Chemical and Biological Threats

When the danger is airborne, your house becomes your best protection, but only if you treat it that way. During my CERT training, we spent considerable time on shelter-in-place procedures for hazmat events, and the principles are simple even if they require some advance preparation.

The goal is to reduce air exchange between inside your home and the outside environment. Modern homes do this reasonably well already, but you can improve the seal significantly with some duct tape and plastic sheeting. I keep a roll of two-inch duct tape and a folded section of plastic sheeting in my home emergency supplies, enough to cover the windows and door gaps in one or two rooms. Pick one interior room with as few windows as possible and seal it from the outside. Tape plastic over windows. Seal the gap under the door with a wet towel and tape the sides. Turn off your HVAC system so it stops pulling outside air in. A sealed room buys you several hours while authorities address the outside threat, which is almost always enough time.

Turning off your HVAC before you seal the room is the step people forget. Your air conditioning system exchanges enormous amounts of air with the outside, and running it during a chemical or biological event negates everything else you do.

Extended Water Storage

The water math for sheltering at home is completely different from bug out bag math. You're not limited to what you can carry on your back. You have time to store, and you have sources that don't exist in the field.

Your water heater holds 40 to 80 gallons of clean, drinkable water right now. Most people don't know this, and almost no one has the equipment to access it during a power outage. A standard hose bib connector and a short length of garden hose lets you drain your water heater into containers. Do this before a long-term emergency rather than after, because once water pressure fails, you can't refill it. Toilet tanks (not bowls) hold another one to two gallons each. During extended stays, rain collection becomes viable if you have suitable containers, and swimming pool water can provide non-drinking water for sanitation with appropriate treatment.

My rule for home water storage is one week of complete supply, minimum, meaning seven gallons per person per week accounting for drinking, cooking, and minimal hygiene — roughly one gallon per person per day. A family of four needs roughly 112 gallons on hand for a two-week self-sufficient stay. Those large stackable water storage containers, the 30 or 55 gallon food-grade plastic drums, are purpose-built for this. I rotate my stored water every six months, using the oldest for laundry or garden irrigation and refilling with fresh.

Food for Extended Stays

Shelter-in-place food planning differs from bug out bag food in one important way: you have a kitchen. You can cook. That changes everything about what you can store and how you manage nutrition over days or weeks.

The mistake most people make is stocking up on strange foods they've never eaten, things that seem practical on paper but cause digestive problems or morale collapse after a few days. During the extended power outage after Milton, the neighbors who did best were eating variations of their normal diet. The ones who struggled were eating foods they'd stockpiled but had never actually tested.

I maintain a two-week rotating pantry of foods I actually eat: canned goods, dried pasta, rice, beans, oats, peanut butter, shelf-stable milk, and cooking staples. Rotation is the key word. I don't maintain a separate emergency food supply that sits unused. I buy extra of what I eat, use the oldest first, and replace it continuously. This way the food is always fresh, always familiar, and always adequate.

A propane camp stove with several extra canisters handles cooking when the power goes out. I tested this during Milton, when we lost electricity for five days. The camp stove managed every meal without any drama. Gas stoves in homes often work fine during power outages since they need only a pilot light or a match, something worth checking before an emergency rather than during one.

Power Management at Home

Power outages during shelter-in-place situations are nearly guaranteed during major events. The difference between a managed extended stay and a miserable ordeal often comes down to how well you've prepared for no electricity.

My home power hierarchy goes: conserve first, then battery backup, then generator if conditions allow. During Milton I ran on battery backup for the first two days before conditions stabilized enough to run a small generator outdoors for a few hours daily to recharge the battery bank and run the refrigerator. A quality battery power station in the 1000 to 2000 watt-hour range will run a CPAP machine, charge all your devices, power fans, and run LED lighting for a day or more on a single charge. These units recharge from a generator, solar panels, or car adapter, and I've tested mine by running it down completely several times to understand its real-world capacity.

Refrigerator management is often overlooked in power planning. A full freezer holds temperature for 48 hours if you keep it closed. Fill empty space with water bottles before a storm hits. Eat refrigerator contents first, then freezer contents, then shelf-stable food. This sequence extends your usable food supply significantly without a generator.

Generator safety gets people killed every year, and most of those deaths are preventable. Generators produce carbon monoxide that accumulates fatally in enclosed spaces. My rule is absolute: the generator runs outside, period. Not in the garage, not on the covered porch, outside with clearance from windows and doors. I lost a neighbor during Milton who made the opposite choice. This is not a rule to bend.

Communication During Shelter-in-Place

When you're staying home, communication priorities shift. You're not trying to coordinate a moving family; you're trying to stay informed and let people know you're okay.

A battery-powered or hand-crank weather radio is the most important communication tool for shelter-in-place scenarios. NOAA weather radio broadcasts continuously and carries official emergency information, evacuation orders, and all-clear notices. During Milton, this was how I tracked the storm's progress when cell service became unreliable. The information was accurate and official, which matters when social media is full of contradictory rumors.

Establish a check-in schedule with one out-of-area contact before any anticipated event. Text messages often get through when voice calls don't because they use less network capacity, so agree on a simple text check-in pattern every 12 hours or so. I had this system in place before Milton and it worked exactly as planned, keeping family members informed about my status while cell networks were congested. Treat everything you see on neighborhood social media as unverified until confirmed by official sources. I've learned to look for official agency accounts and local emergency management posts rather than relying on neighborhood groups, where panic and misinformation spread faster than facts.

Mental Health During Extended Confinement

Nobody talks much about what happens to people psychologically during extended stays at home, but it's where a lot of shelter-in-place situations actually break down. The physical supplies hold out. The power management works. But the psychological stress of confinement, uncertainty, and disrupted routine erodes people's ability to function.

I went through five days of confinement during Milton without electricity, without the ability to leave safely, and on my own. The physical challenges were manageable. The psychological challenge was real, and it required deliberate management. Routine matters more than almost anything else during confinement. Waking at the same time, eating at regular intervals, maintaining some structure to the day. I had a loose daily schedule during those five days that divided time into useful work, rest, and something like entertainment. It sounds trivial when you write it down, but it made an enormous difference in how clearly I could think and how well I held up.

Having something to do is not a luxury during confinement, it's a psychological requirement. Books, card games, puzzles, a project you've been putting off, anything that gives your mind something to work on besides the emergency. I was actually somewhat productive during Milton, reorganizing my emergency supply inventory and reading two books I'd been meaning to get to. Physical movement matters even in confined spaces. Stretching, basic exercises, walking around your home regularly, all help manage the anxiety that builds during uncertainty. The worst thing you can do is sit still for hours watching storm coverage on your phone.

Knowing When to Leave

Sheltering in place only works until it doesn't. The decision to leave mid-event can be more dangerous than either staying or having left early, so understanding your triggers for abandoning shelter is something to think through before you need to act on it.

My triggers are structural: if the building is compromised or becoming dangerous, you leave regardless of what's outside. If fire threatens the structure. If rising water enters the living space and continues to rise. If a medical emergency requires professional care. These aren't situations where you reassess, they're pre-decided actions. During Milton, the challenge was complete darkness outside during peak storm conditions. Leaving would have required walking through debris-covered streets in 100 mph wind gusts toward no clear destination. The building held. That was the right call. But I'd thought through in advance what would make me leave, and I knew where I would go.

Your bug out bag plays a direct role in shelter-in-place scenarios because if you do have to leave mid-event, you grab the bag and go. The bag sitting by the door isn't just your planned departure kit, it's your exit capability for any scenario. Pre-identify your destination before you commit to sheltering in place. Which nearby building has the strongest construction? Which community shelter is within walking distance? What's the route if you have to travel on foot in the dark? Answer these questions during your normal planning, not during the emergency.

Chapter 16: What to Wear

Why Clothing Gets Left Out of Bug Out Bag Guides

Most bug out bag guides skip clothing or deal with it in a paragraph. I've never understood this. Clothing is the one piece of emergency equipment you wear continuously, it's your primary interface with the environment, and getting it wrong can kill you faster than almost any other mistake you make. If you're soaked and cold because you packed the wrong jacket, it doesn't matter how good your water filter is.

I learned this through two separate miserable experiences. The first was that mountain hike where I got caught in unexpected rain in a cotton t-shirt and jeans, which turned the second half of the hike into a hypothermia risk management exercise. The second was the aftermath of the Northridge earthquake, when I spent a full day outdoors in whatever I'd grabbed in the dark, which happened to be completely wrong for the weather and the physical work we were doing. Neither situation was life-threatening, but both taught me that clothing deserves the same systematic attention as water and food.

The Foundation: Footwear and Socks

Start with your feet because your feet determine whether you can move at all. My wife's barefoot run across broken glass during the earthquake is the reason I now sleep with shoes within arm's reach of my bed. Foot protection is the single piece of clothing that can become urgent within seconds of an emergency beginning.

The shoes in your bug out bag should be sturdy, broken-in hiking boots or trail shoes with ankle support, not sneakers and definitely not sandals. Broken-in matters. A pair of stiff new boots that you've never walked in will give you blisters within a mile. I rotate my hiking boots into everyday use a few months before retiring them to emergency kit status, so by the time they're in the bag they're already shaped to my feet.

Pack three pairs of wool or synthetic socks for a 72-hour kit. Not cotton. Cotton holds moisture against your skin and causes blisters faster than almost anything else. Wool and synthetic fabrics wick moisture away and maintain some insulating value even when wet. During extended hiking in the Sierra Nevada I switched from cotton to wool socks and the difference in foot comfort was dramatic enough that I've never gone back. Two pairs minimum, three preferred, and change socks daily even if you can't wash them. A dry sock against your foot is more important than a clean one.

The Layering System

I covered layering philosophy in Chapter 5 but didn't specify what to actually pack, so here it is. Three layers handle everything from desert heat to mountain cold when you choose them right.

The base layer sits against your skin and its only job is moisture management. Synthetic fabrics like polyester or merino wool both work well. Merino is more comfortable and less odor-prone over multiple days, which matters when you can't do laundry. Synthetic is cheaper and dries faster. Either is correct. What's wrong is cotton, for the same reason it's wrong for socks. Pack two base layer tops and two pairs of base layer bottoms so you have a dry set to sleep in while the worn set airs out.

The insulating layer traps warm air against your body. A lightweight fleece jacket or a down puffy is the right choice here. Down packs smaller and insulates better by weight, but it loses nearly all its insulating value when wet and takes forever to dry. Synthetic insulation is heavier but works when wet and dries faster. If you're in a climate that gets rain, lean synthetic. If you're in dry desert or mountain terrain, down is fine. One insulating jacket is sufficient because it doesn't get wet against your skin.

The outer layer blocks wind and rain. This is where people most often go wrong by buying cheap rain ponchos. Ponchos are better than nothing but they pool water, catch wind like a sail, and make any physical activity miserable. A proper rain jacket with a hood, pit zips for ventilation, and a waterproof-breathable membrane costs more but performs like a different category of product. You need one that fits over your insulating layer without being so baggy it catches wind. Test this fit before you buy by trying the jacket on over a fleece in the store.

Pants, Gloves, and Head Coverage

One pair of durable pants that you're already wearing plus one backup pair covers most situations. Hiking pants in a synthetic or nylon-blend fabric dry fast, resist abrasion, and move well under a pack. Jeans are a poor emergency choice despite being nearly universal. They're heavy, take forever to dry, and when wet they're cold and chafe badly over distance. I wore jeans through the earthquake aftermath and by the end of the day they were abrading my inner thighs. Convertible pants that zip off into shorts add versatility for minimal extra weight and are worth considering for warmer climates.

Work gloves often get left out entirely and shouldn't be. Moving debris, climbing over rubble, handling sharp materials, or building shelter all damage your hands quickly if they're unprotected. A pair of leather work gloves or cut-resistant synthetic gloves weighs almost nothing and takes up minimal space. I keep a pair in the top pocket of my bag where I can reach them without unpacking anything. My hands have taken enough damage from unplanned work that I've stopped thinking of gloves as optional.

A wool or fleece knit hat and a lightweight sun hat cover opposite ends of the temperature spectrum and together weigh about four ounces. The knit hat matters more than most people expect because heat loss from an uncovered head in cold wind is significant. The sun hat matters in desert and hot climates where hours of direct sun exposure can cause both sunburn and heat illness. I also keep a lightweight balaclava that can serve as a neck gaiter in moderate cold or a full face covering in extreme conditions. These three items handle every head and face situation I've encountered across three decades of outdoor emergencies.

Seasonal Swaps and Regional Adjustments

The clothing kit I just described is a baseline for a temperate climate with variable conditions. If you live in Florida like I do now, your insulation needs are minimal but your sun and rain protection needs are much greater. I swapped my down puffy for a lightweight windbreaker and added a long-sleeved sun shirt. If you're in Minnesota, your insulating layer should be heavier and you should add waterproof over-pants and insulated gloves. The framework stays the same. What changes is the weight and rating of each layer.

Review and rotate clothing in your bag twice a year. Children outgrow their emergency clothing faster than adults. Body weight changes affect fit. And clothing that's sat compressed in a pack for a year may have degraded elastic or developed mildew you won't notice until you put it on during an emergency. The clothing review takes fifteen minutes and is worth every one of them.

Chapter 17: Cooking Systems

The Hot Water Problem

Chapter 3 walked through emergency food selection, and several of the best options on that list, freeze-dried meals, instant oatmeal, dehydrated soups, hot coffee, require one thing: boiling water. Chapter 2 mentioned boiling as a water purification method. But neither chapter addressed the obvious question that follows from both: how do you actually produce heat in the field when the power is out and you're working from a bag?

The answer depends on your situation. I've used every type of portable stove across three decades of hiking and emergency situations, and each has genuine tradeoffs that matter differently depending on whether you're on foot, sheltering in a vehicle, or set up at a base camp for several days. Understanding those tradeoffs lets you choose the right system rather than defaulting to whatever is cheapest or whatever some website is selling this week.

Canister Stoves

Canister stoves run on pressurized isobutane-propane canisters and are the system I reach for most often. They screw directly onto a standard canister, ignite with a push-button piezo lighter, and boil a liter of water in about three minutes. Setup takes ten seconds. Cleanup is nonexistent. When I was managing a five-day power outage alone after Milton, my canister stove handled every hot meal and every pot of coffee without a single problem.

The main limitation is cold weather performance. Isobutane-propane mixtures lose pressure in cold temperatures, which means output drops significantly when it's below freezing and can stop entirely in very cold conditions. If you're in a cold climate, keep your canisters in your sleeping bag overnight and warm them in your hands before use. You can also buy cold-weather blended fuels that perform better at low temperatures. The second limitation is that you can't see how much fuel is left in a canister. Weigh them when full and mark the full weight on the canister with a marker, then weigh them periodically during use to gauge remaining fuel. A small canister typically boils around twelve liters before running empty, which is roughly four days of minimal cooking for one person.

Alcohol Stoves

Alcohol stoves are the ultralight option. The stove itself is often a small titanium or aluminum cup that burns denatured alcohol or HEET fuel additive. They weigh almost nothing, the fuel is available at most hardware stores and some gas stations, and there are no moving parts to break. I used an alcohol stove for a solid year of weekend backpacking and it handled everything from coffee to full hot meals.

The downsides are real. Alcohol stoves are slow, taking eight to ten minutes to boil a liter compared to three minutes for a canister stove. They perform poorly in wind without a dedicated windscreen. The flame is nearly invisible in daylight, which creates a burn hazard when you're not paying attention. And they don't simmer well, they run at full output until the fuel runs out. For emergency situations where speed matters and conditions may be suboptimal, these limitations add up. Alcohol stoves are best suited to planned, methodical cooking in calm conditions, which is not always what emergencies provide.

Solid Fuel Tablets

Esbit tablets and similar solid fuel cubes are the backup-to-the-backup option. They're cheap, extremely light, compact, and have an indefinite shelf life when kept dry. A single tablet burns for about twelve minutes at sufficient heat to boil water with a suitable pot. They don't require a separate stove, just a folding stand or a few rocks to hold your pot above the flame.

I keep a dozen tablets in my bug out bag as a third-tier backup regardless of what primary stove system I'm carrying. The tablets leave a sticky residue on pots and produce a faint chemical smell that transfers to food, which limits their appeal for regular cooking. But in a scenario where my primary and backup stove systems have both failed and I need hot water to treat water or warm someone who is hypothermic, those tablets could be critical. They're also useful for fire starting in wet conditions since they light reliably and burn hot enough to ignite damp wood.

Cookware and Setup

The stove is only part of the system. You need something to cook in. A titanium or hard-anodized aluminum pot in the one-liter range handles everything from boiling water to reconstituting meals to heating soup. Titanium is lighter and more durable but expensive. Aluminum is heavier but cheap and readily available. I carry a simple 900ml aluminum pot that nests around my canister stove and stashes two fuel canisters and a lighter inside it, making the whole cooking kit a single compact unit about the size of a large coffee mug.

A windscreen makes an enormous difference in fuel efficiency and cooking speed regardless of which stove system you use. Wind strips heat away from the pot and forces your stove to work much harder to accomplish the same result. A simple reflective windscreen cut from heavy-duty aluminum foil weighs almost nothing and can cut your fuel consumption by thirty to forty percent in moderate wind. Don't use a windscreen so close around a canister stove that it reflects heat back onto the canister, though, because pressurized canisters can rupture if they overheat. Keep the windscreen around the pot, not encircling the whole stove.

The eating tools that come with most camping cookware sets are adequate but add unnecessary weight. A single long-handled titanium spoon handles every eating task you'll encounter with emergency rations. A folding camp knife completes the kit. Skip the fork unless you have strong feelings about it. During the days after the Northridge earthquake, we ate every meal with whatever utensils we could grab from the kitchen before leaving. It worked fine. The psychological desire for proper cutlery is real but it doesn't translate into any actual functional need once you're eating reconstituted camping meals from a single pot.

Chapter 18: Signaling and Being Found

The Problem Nobody Plans For

Most bug out bag planning focuses on self-rescue: getting out, getting to safety, surviving until conditions improve. What gets almost no attention is the scenario where you can't self-rescue and need to be found. You're injured. You're pinned under debris. You're stranded in terrain you can't exit under your own power. In all of these situations, your survival depends not on what you can do, but on how effectively you can communicate your presence and location to people who are trying to find you.

During the mountain rescue when my father had his apparent heart attack in that canyon, I left him and climbed out to get help. Before I left, I marked my route with rocks and broken branches, both so the rescue team could follow my path down to him and so I could find him again in the dark if I needed to return. Improvised trail marking is low-tech signaling, but it's the same underlying principle as everything in this chapter: you make yourself findable when you can't come to the rescuers, so they can come to you.

The Whistle

A quality emergency whistle produces sound that carries much farther than a human voice and requires a fraction of the energy. You can blow a whistle for hours after your voice has given out completely. In a search and rescue scenario, rescuers listen for signals, and three blasts is the universal signal for distress in most systems. A whistle attached to the outside of your bag or clipped to your jacket strap is always within reach, including when everything else is inaccessible.

Not all whistles are equal. Pealess whistles, meaning those without a ball bearing inside the chamber, work in freezing temperatures and when wet, while traditional whistles with peas can stick or stop working entirely in cold conditions. I carry a Fox 40 pealess whistle that I first used during CERT training.

During a search and rescue exercise, we tested different whistle types in rain, and the pealess models outperformed the traditional ones significantly in both reliability and volume. The difference in audible range in field conditions was enough that the choice was obvious. A good pealess whistle costs under five dollars, weighs half an ounce, and should be on your bag's exterior where you can grab it without opening anything.

Signal Mirrors

A signal mirror can be seen from aircraft at distances that seem impossible until you've tested one. In direct sunlight, a properly aimed signal mirror produces a flash visible for ten miles or more, which is beyond the effective range of any sound-based signal. During daylight search operations where aircraft are involved, nothing else comes close to this range.

Military-spec glass signal mirrors have a sighting hole in the center that lets you aim the reflected beam with precision. You hold the mirror close to your face, look through the sighting hole, and move the mirror until you see the reflected sunlight land on your target. It sounds complicated and is slightly awkward at first, but with twenty minutes of practice in your backyard it becomes second nature. I practiced this during a hiking trip after the mountain incident with my father, using a ridge line as my target. Within a few attempts I was landing the flash accurately at distances of over a mile.

An actual signal mirror costs about eight dollars and is worth every cent over improvised alternatives like a phone screen or the back of a CD. Those alternatives work in a pinch but produce far less reflective output and are much harder to aim. The glass mirror goes in the top lid pocket of my bag alongside the whistle, accessible without opening the main compartment.

Chemical Light Sticks

Chem lights, the glow sticks that you crack to activate, are useful for nighttime signaling and marking. They produce a steady, omnidirectional glow that requires no batteries, produces no heat, and continues working even if they get wet or are submerged. Hung from a tree above your position during a night search operation, a chem light makes you visible from a significant distance without requiring you to do anything once it's activated.

During CERT training we used chem lights extensively for marking hazards, indicating safe passages through debris, and marking the location of injured people waiting for extraction. The color coding matters in organized rescue operations: green typically means all clear or safe passage, red marks hazards or indicates a fatality, yellow marks a location requiring attention. If you're the one being found rather than the one doing the finding, the color matters less than having something visible at all. I keep four chem lights in my bag, two green and two red, which covers most signaling and marking needs for a 72-hour period.

Shelf life is the one genuine maintenance issue with chem lights. They have a typical shelf life of two to four years and will produce reduced output or fail completely past that point. Mark the purchase date on yours and replace them during your biannual inventory check. The cost is negligible, about a dollar each in bulk, so there's no reason to keep expired ones in your kit.

Personal Locator Beacons

If you spend significant time in remote areas or your likely evacuation routes include wilderness terrain, a personal locator beacon is worth serious consideration. These devices, commonly called PLBs, transmit your GPS coordinates to search and rescue satellites when activated. The signal reaches emergency services regardless of cell coverage, radio range, or atmospheric conditions. Registration is free and required, activation is a single button, and they require no subscription. A PLB is a last-resort device, meaning you activate it when you need rescue rather than as a routine communication tool, but in that last-resort moment it can cut rescue response time from days to hours.

Chapter 4 covered satellite messengers like the Garmin inReach, which offer two-way communication and GPS tracking in addition to rescue signaling. If you can afford one and will carry it consistently, a satellite messenger is the more capable device. A PLB is the simpler, cheaper option for people whose primary concern is rescue capability without the ongoing subscription cost. Either is far better than nothing when you're in terrain where no other signal reaches.

Chapter 19: What to Carry on Your Person

The Bag You Can't Leave Behind

The forest fire that trapped me on the mountain road between Lake Arrowhead and San Bernardino didn't give me time to go home and get my bug out bag. I was in my car, on a road I drove regularly, on what had started as a completely ordinary day. The fire moved faster than anyone expected, cut the road behind me, and suddenly I was sitting in a vehicle surrounded by burning trees with nothing except what was already in my car and on my body.

That experience taught me something that took years to fully integrate into my preparedness thinking: your bug out bag is only useful if you have access to it. A perfectly packed bag sitting in your hall closet is worthless when you are trapped on a mountain road, stranded at work during an earthquake, or caught in any emergency that separates you from home. What you carry on your body every single day, without exception, is the preparedness layer that is always with you. Everything else is a supplement to that foundation.

Every day carry, commonly called EDC, is the practice of carrying a consistent set of tools and supplies on your person as a matter of daily habit. The goal is not to carry a miniature bug out bag in your pockets. The goal is to carry the small number of items that provide immediate capability for the most common emergencies while being compact and unobtrusive enough to carry genuinely every day. An EDC kit that is too heavy or bulky gets left behind on the days you decide it's inconvenient, which defeats the entire purpose.

The Core Five

After decades of refining what I carry daily, I have settled on five categories that every adult should have on their person at all times. Everything else is optional and situational. These five are not.

Light. A keychain or pocket LED light small enough to forget you're carrying it. Modern micro-lights produce useful illumination from a device the size of a large coin. The Streamlight Nano and similar lights run for hours on a watch battery and weigh almost nothing. The argument for carrying a dedicated light rather than relying on your phone's flashlight is that your phone may be dead, broken, or needed for communication at the moment you need light. A dedicated light costs under twenty dollars and adds nothing meaningful to your daily carry weight. On the mountain road in the fire, the firefighter who jumped into my car had a light clipped to his gear. When the smoke reduced visibility and I needed to read my gauges and controls clearly, that light mattered.

Cutting tool. A folding knife or a multi-tool small enough to pocket without discomfort. The cutting edge solves problems that nothing else in your pocket can solve: cutting a seatbelt after an accident, opening packaging, cutting cordage, preparing food, and dozens of other tasks that come up regularly in both emergencies and ordinary life. A small Swiss Army Knife, a Benchmade Mini Bugout, or a compact Leatherman Micra all work. The specific tool matters less than having something sharp, reliable, and legal in your jurisdiction that you actually carry every day. Check local laws, especially if you travel frequently, because blade length and locking blade restrictions vary.

Fire. A lighter. A basic Bic lighter fits in any pocket, costs a dollar, and provides fire starting capability in almost any conditions. Fire addresses warmth, signaling, water purification, and cooking. It also provides psychological comfort during emergencies in a way that is hard to overstate until you have needed it. The mountain road experience was terrifying in ways that have nothing to do with the physical danger. Having the ability to make fire, to do something active and constructive, matters to human psychology under stress. A lighter in your pocket at all times costs nothing and weighs nothing.

Communication. A charged phone with emergency contacts stored and key offline maps downloaded. The phone is not just a phone. It is your navigation system, your weather alert receiver, your contact with family members, your ability to call for help, and your access to critical information. The discipline of keeping it charged is part of emergency preparedness. A phone that dies at two in the afternoon because you did not plug it in the night before is not an emergency tool. Carry a small power bank if your phone does not reliably last the day. The phone is your most important EDC item for most emergencies and the one people take most for granted.

Cash. A small amount of physical cash in your wallet, separate from what you might need for normal spending. Fifty dollars in mixed denominations, tucked behind other cards where it will not be spent casually, is enough to handle basic emergency needs: food, fuel, a bus ticket, a phone call, or a tip to someone who helps you. As Chapter 9 covered in more detail, electronic payment systems fail during power outages and network disruptions. The cash habit costs nothing if you never need it and solves real problems if you do.

Expanding the Daily Carry

Beyond the core five, several additional items add meaningful capability with minimal burden for people who spend time outdoors, commute long distances, or live in higher-risk environments.

A whistle clipped to a keychain or zipper pull adds signaling capability that weighs under half an ounce. As Chapter 18 covered, a pealess whistle carries farther than your voice and functions when you cannot yell. A paracord bracelet or a small length of paracord in your pocket adds cordage for repairs, improvised lashing, or emergency use. A small packet of water purification tablets in a pocket or wallet provides the ability to make almost any water source drinkable if you find yourself without other options for long enough. A space blanket folded into a credit-card-sized packet fits in a wallet and provides emergency thermal protection that weighs less than an ounce. Individual bandages and a small packet of pain medication in a wallet slot handle the most common minor medical needs without requiring a full first aid kit.

For people who carry a bag, backpack, or purse daily, the EDC expands further: a full-size portable power bank, a larger folding knife or multi-tool, a proper pocket first aid kit, a granola bar or other compact food, and a small water bottle. A bag that goes with you every day to work or school can bridge meaningfully between your pocket EDC and your full bug out bag. The question to ask about any item you consider adding is whether you will genuinely carry it every single day, including inconvenient days. If the answer is no, it does not belong in your EDC.

The Get-Home Mindset

The purpose of personal EDC in an emergency context is often described as a "get-home kit," meaning the supplies that allow you to travel from wherever you are when an emergency occurs back to your home, your vehicle, or your bug out bag. This framing is useful because it focuses the purpose clearly: not survival for three days, but the ability to navigate an unexpected situation and reach better resources.

Think through the scenarios most relevant to your daily life. If you commute by train, an earthquake that shuts down the transit system could leave you several miles from home on foot. If you work in a high-rise, a structural emergency could require walking down many flights of stairs and then covering distance on foot in business clothing. If you travel frequently for work, you may regularly find yourself in unfamiliar cities when something happens. Each of these scenarios has slightly different EDC implications, but the core five handle the fundamentals in all of them. The rest is calibration to your specific situation.

Chapter 20: Your Vehicle as an Emergency Resource

The Emergency Resource You Drive Every Day

When the fire closed the road behind me on that mountain, my car became my emergency shelter, my communication attempt, and my primary protection from the fire around me. It also had almost nothing useful in it beyond standard factory equipment. That afternoon sitting in smoke watching trees burn, wishing I had water, a better flashlight, and a way to signal beyond my car horn, taught me that a vehicle is not just transportation. In any emergency that occurs away from home, your car is often your first and most immediate resource, and most cars are as unprepared as I was that day.

Chapter 12 addressed vehicle bug out bags as part of a multiple-bag strategy. This chapter goes deeper, treating the vehicle itself as an emergency platform and covering what every vehicle should carry regardless of whether a dedicated bug out bag is also present. These are the supplies that live in your car permanently, that you maintain without thinking about, and that will be there whether you are commuting to work, driving to the grocery store, or evacuating ahead of a hurricane.

Vehicle Mechanical Preparedness

A vehicle that breaks down during an emergency evacuation is worse than not having a vehicle, because it blocks the road for others, strands you in potentially dangerous conditions, and consumes rescue resources that are already stretched thin. The most common breakdowns that strand people are the most preventable: flat tires, dead batteries, and running out of fuel. Each has a simple solution that costs almost nothing to maintain.

A full-size spare tire, not a compact spare, is worth having if your vehicle accommodates one. Compact spares, the narrow temporary tires sometimes called donuts, are rated for limited speeds and distances and are not appropriate for extended emergency travel or rough terrain. If your vehicle came with a compact spare, know its rated limitations and seriously consider whether upgrading to a full-size spare makes sense for your emergency preparedness. A hydraulic floor jack and a breaker bar in addition to the factory tire iron make changing a tire feasible on your own rather than requiring a service call that will not come quickly during a mass emergency.

Jump-start capability is the solution to a dead battery, which is among the most common reasons people are stranded. A quality lithium jump starter, the portable battery pack style rather than cables that require another vehicle, fits in a glove compartment and can start a car engine multiple times on a single charge. These devices cost between fifty and one hundred dollars and have replaced jumper cables as the practical choice because they do not require another vehicle to be present. Keep it charged. Check it every few months. Mine has started my car on three separate occasions over the years and has been worth the price each time.

Fuel management is the preparedness habit that most directly determines whether you can evacuate at all. During Milton, people who waited until the evacuation order to fill their tanks sat in lines for hours at stations that ran dry before they reached the pump. I had a standing rule during hurricane season: the tank does not go below half. This rule costs nothing. It requires slightly more frequent fueling stops on an irregular schedule. It means that when an evacuation order comes, I get in the car and go rather than spending the first thirty minutes of my evacuation window competing for fuel with everyone else who waited. In California wildfire situations, where evacuation orders can come with minutes rather than hours of warning, this rule is even more important.

Basic fluids and maintenance items round out vehicle mechanical preparedness: a quart of the correct motor oil for your engine, coolant, and windshield washer fluid stored in the trunk. A tow strap rated for your vehicle's weight, which costs about twenty dollars and stores flat, allows another vehicle to pull you out of mud, shallow water, or a ditch. A folding shovel is useful for digging out in sand, snow, or mud. A set of traction boards, the plastic devices that go under a stuck tire, is the most effective tool for self-recovery in soft surfaces and is worth the trunk space if you drive in areas with sand, snow, or loose soil.

Water and Food in the Vehicle

A minimum of one gallon of water per person who regularly rides in the vehicle, stored in the trunk in sealed containers, is the baseline. This covers a breakdown in hot weather, an extended traffic delay during an evacuation, or a medical situation requiring hydration. In Florida summer heat, the inside of a parked car reaches temperatures that degrade plastic containers and promote bacterial growth faster than in cooler climates. I use stainless steel containers or thick-walled HDPE jugs rather than standard bottled water, which degrades faster in heat, and I rotate the water every three months regardless of condition.

A small supply of compact, heat-stable food in the trunk covers extended delays and short separations from your main food supply. Energy bars, nuts, and jerky rotate well and tolerate vehicle temperature extremes better than most food. Test your chosen products by leaving them in your car through one full summer cycle before committing to them as your vehicle food supply. I learned from experience that some energy bars I thought were heat-stable turned into unusable messes after a summer in a Florida trunk. What survives that environment is what earns a permanent spot in the vehicle kit.

Safety and Signaling Equipment

A vehicle accident or breakdown creates an immediate signaling need: letting other drivers know you are there, and letting rescue know where you are. The factory hazard lights handle the first need while the battery lasts. Beyond that, you need independent signaling capability.

LED road flares have replaced traditional flares as the smart choice for vehicle kits. They are reusable, last for hours on a charge, produce no combustion risk, and work in rain and wind that would extinguish a traditional flare. Set them behind and to the sides of a stopped vehicle to create a visible warning zone for approaching traffic. Three LED flares, stored in the trunk and recharged annually, handle almost any roadside emergency scenario. Reflective triangles are the alternative that requires no batteries and stores completely flat, though they are less visible than flares in daylight.

A bright flashlight dedicated to the vehicle, separate from the one in your EDC, handles situations where you need to see under the hood, change a tire in the dark, or signal from distance. Mount it somewhere accessible from the driver's seat rather than buried in the trunk where it is hard to reach during an emergency. A crank or solar-charged emergency radio in the vehicle glove compartment provides weather and emergency alert information independently of the phone and without draining the car battery.

A window breaker and seatbelt cutter, sold as a combined tool for about ten dollars, belongs clipped to the driver's sun visor or door pocket, not in the glove compartment or trunk. If you go into water or the door jams after an accident, you need this tool immediately and you need it accessible with one hand. This is one of the items most people intend to buy and never get around to. Buy it this week and put it somewhere you can reach with your seatbelt on. The mountain road fire and every other emergency I have experienced confirms the same principle: the tool in your hand when you need it is the only tool that counts.

First Aid and Comfort in the Vehicle

A more complete first aid kit belongs in the vehicle than in your pocket EDC, because the vehicle gives you the space for it. A vehicle first aid kit should include everything in the pocket first aid kit plus a tourniquet, a pressure bandage, hemostatic gauze for serious bleeding control, a CPR face shield, nitrile gloves, trauma shears, and a foil space blanket. Vehicle accidents are among the most common causes of serious injury in the country, and the minutes before emergency services arrive are when the contents of a vehicle first aid kit matter most. A Stop the Bleed kit, which is designed for controlling life-threatening hemorrhage, is a worthwhile addition and is available pre-assembled for around thirty dollars.

Comfort items in the vehicle matter more than people expect during extended emergencies. A lightweight blanket or two covers everyone in the vehicle if you are stranded overnight in cold weather, waiting out a storm, or dealing with shock after an accident. A change of clothes sealed in a bag, appropriate for the current season, covers the situation where you are caught away from home and your clothes are damaged, soaked, or contaminated. Hand sanitizer, wet wipes, toilet paper, and a small trowel handle sanitation needs during extended roadside stops when facilities are not available. These are not luxuries, they are the supplies that determine whether an extended vehicle emergency is merely unpleasant or becomes a health problem.

Climate-Specific Vehicle Considerations

Florida and hot climate vehicles need summer-specific items: a reflective windshield sun shade that also serves as a signaling device, extra water beyond the baseline given the speed at which heat exhaustion develops in extreme heat, and electrolyte packets for extended heat exposure. Cooling towels, the chemical evaporative type, provide meaningful temperature reduction without requiring ice. A battery-powered fan provides airflow when the engine cannot run. The inside of a vehicle in Florida summer sun can reach temperatures lethal to children and pets within minutes, which is also relevant to how you store medications and anything temperature-sensitive in your vehicle kit.

Cold climate vehicles need winter-specific additions: an ice scraper and snow brush, a bag of sand or cat litter for traction under stuck tires, traction boards or chains depending on the terrain, extra warm clothing and blankets beyond what you might otherwise carry, and hand warmers. A folding shovel capable of moving snow serves double duty for digging out a stuck vehicle and for general emergency use. A candle in a metal container is a low-tech heat source that can meaningfully warm a vehicle interior for hours, consuming very little oxygen and providing more warmth than most people expect from a single flame.

The Vehicle as Evacuation Platform

When a vehicle becomes part of an evacuation rather than just a breakdown scenario, the priorities shift. You are no longer waiting for help, you are moving toward a destination with everything you need to sustain yourself and your family for multiple days. The vehicle kit and the bug out bag work together as a system: the bug out bag handles what you need if you have to leave the vehicle on foot, and the vehicle kit handles what you need while you are in it.

Load the vehicle systematically when evacuating rather than throwing things in randomly. Items you may need to access during the drive go in the passenger compartment. Items you will not need until you reach a destination go in the trunk. Your bug out bag goes in a position where you can grab it quickly if you have to abandon the vehicle. Cash, medications, and critical documents travel with you in the passenger compartment, not in bags buried in the trunk.

Know your vehicle's range on a full tank and plan fuel stops before you need them rather than when the gauge demands it. During evacuations, gas stations in the immediate area of the disaster often close or run dry within hours of an evacuation order. The first fuel stop you plan should be far enough outside the evacuation zone that it is unlikely to have the same shortages. Know alternate routes to that stop in case the primary route is gridlocked or closed.

After the mountain road fire, the firefighter who saved my life did so because he was prepared for exactly that kind of situation with the gear and training to address it. I drove away from that mountain road with my life and almost nothing else. Everything in this chapter is the result of thirty-plus years of not wanting to be that unprepared again when it matters.

Chapter 21: The Medication Kit

Why Medications Live Outside the Bug Out Bag

Chapter 6 covered the general principle of keeping prescription medications stocked for emergencies. This chapter covers the system I actually use, because the principle and the practice are different enough to warrant a separate discussion.

I keep my emergency medications in a dedicated, clearly labeled box in a kitchen cupboard, completely separate from my bug out bag. Not inside the bag, not next to the bag, but in its own location that I check independently on a monthly schedule. When I evacuate, I grab the bug out bag with one hand and the medication kit with the other. They travel together but they live separately, and that distinction is intentional.

The reason is expiration management. Prescription medications expire and must be replaced on a cycle that has nothing to do with the rest of your emergency supplies. If your medications live inside your bug out bag, they get checked on the same biannual schedule as everything else, which is not frequent enough for many drugs. Monthly checks, which is what my medication kit gets, require easy access and a system that makes inspection quick. Digging through a packed bag every month to verify drug dates is friction that leads to the check being skipped. A dedicated box in a cupboard takes thirty seconds to open and inspect.

The second reason is that medications need different storage conditions than most emergency gear. Most emergency supplies tolerate a range of temperatures and humidity levels. Many medications do not. Keeping the medication kit in an interior kitchen cupboard, away from the heat and humidity extremes of a garage or the direct sun that can reach a hall closet, gives them better storage conditions than they would get packed into the bag.

What Goes in the Kit

The medication kit contains a 30-day supply of every prescription medication I take whenever I can achieve it, with a hard minimum of one week. Thirty days is the target because it covers the realistic duration of most regional emergencies, gives you time to reach medical resources without pressure, and is achievable for most maintenance medications with some advance planning. One week is the floor below which I will not let the kit fall, because a week is enough to reach a pharmacy, a shelter with medical staff, or a situation where I can get a new prescription filled. If you genuinely cannot maintain a 30-day supply given your medications and insurance, one week maintained and current beats 30 days sitting expired. But work toward 30 days, and here is why that goal is more achievable than most people realize.

Prescription medications go in their original labeled bottles whenever possible, or in clearly labeled weekly pill organizers with the prescription information written on a card stored with them. Original bottles matter because they identify the medication, dosage, prescribing physician, and pharmacy, all information that emergency medical personnel need if you cannot communicate clearly. A first responder who finds you unconscious with a clearly labeled bottle of metoprolol understands your cardiac history immediately. The same responder finding unlabeled pills has nothing to work with.

Over-the-counter medications in the kit cover the most common medical needs that arise during emergencies and extended displacement: ibuprofen and acetaminophen for pain and fever, an antihistamine for allergic reactions, an anti-diarrheal, an antacid, a decongestant, throat lozenges, and a topical antibiotic ointment. None of these are exotic and all of them address problems that become genuinely disruptive during an emergency when you cannot simply run to a drugstore. During the days after the Northridge earthquake, a simple headache became a significant problem for people who had nothing to treat it with. After Milton, the neighbor whose stomach illness during the power outage would have been a minor inconvenience in normal times became a serious concern because she had nothing to manage it and could not easily get to a pharmacy.

A printed medication list lives in the kit as a separate document. One copy goes in the kit itself, a second goes in the documentation section of the bug out bag, and a third stays in my wallet. The list includes every medication, the dose, the frequency, what it treats, the prescribing doctor and their contact number, and the pharmacy information. This list exists for two scenarios: someone else needing to manage my medications on my behalf, and me needing to get emergency refills from an unfamiliar physician or pharmacy that has no access to my records.

The Monthly Check

On the first of every month, I open the medication kit and check every item. The check takes less than five minutes and covers three things: expiration dates, quantity, and condition. Anything expiring within sixty days gets rotated into my current daily supply and replaced with fresh medication from my next prescription fill. Anything below the target quantity gets restocked. Anything showing signs of degradation, discoloration, unusual odor, or damaged packaging gets replaced regardless of the expiration date.

The sixty-day buffer on expiration is not arbitrary. It gives me two full monthly check cycles to notice an upcoming expiration and arrange a replacement before the medication is actually expired. If I catch something expiring at sixty days and my next check is in thirty days, I still have thirty days after that to get a refill. If I only checked for medications expiring in the next thirty days, I would need to act immediately every time I found something, which is not always possible.

Getting your doctor and insurance company to cooperate with this system under normal circumstances requires a direct conversation. Most insurance plans will not fill a prescription early without medical justification. The justification, in this case, is legitimate: you are maintaining an emergency supply and need a small buffer beyond your standard monthly fill. Many physicians will document this in your chart, and most insurance plans will accommodate it once the reason is explained. Some medications, especially controlled substances, have tighter restrictions that make maintaining an emergency supply more complicated. Work with your prescribing physician on those specifically.

When a Disaster Is Declared, the Rules Change

One of the most useful and least-known facts in emergency medication planning is that a governor's emergency declaration substantially relaxes the normal rules around prescription refills. Understanding this doesn't replace having your own supply, but it changes how you think about what happens once a major disaster is officially declared.

Florida has some of the clearest emergency pharmacy law in the country, which I learned in detail after Milton. Under Florida Statute §252.358, when the governor issues a state of emergency declaration, all health insurers and managed care organizations are required to waive time restrictions on early refills for the duration of the emergency. That means the "too soon to refill" restriction that normally prevents you from getting a refill before your current supply runs down disappears entirely. You can walk into a pharmacy and refill your maintenance medications immediately, regardless of when you last filled them, and your insurance must cover it.

Under Florida Statute §465.0275, pharmacists can go further than that. If a pharmacist cannot readily reach your prescriber for refill authorization, they can dispense up to a 30-day supply of any maintenance medication essential to treating a chronic condition without a new prescription. This covers most of the common medications people depend on daily: blood pressure medications, diabetes drugs, thyroid medications, cholesterol medications, psychiatric medications, and similar maintenance drugs. The pharmacist documents the dispensing and notifies your regular prescriber afterward.

Controlled substances have more complexity. Under Florida emergency orders, Schedule III, IV, and V controlled substances, which include many commonly prescribed medications for anxiety, sleep, and pain, can also be refilled early. Schedule II drugs, the most tightly regulated class including stimulants like Adderall and opioids like oxycodone, remain restricted to their normal rules even during declared emergencies. If you depend on a Schedule II medication, maintaining your own adequate supply ahead of any emergency becomes even more critical, because you cannot rely on emergency provisions to fill the gap.

Other states have similar emergency pharmacy provisions, though the specifics vary. Most states allow pharmacists to dispense 30-day emergency supplies of non-controlled maintenance medications under governor's emergency declarations, with 72 hours to seven days typically allowed for Schedule III–V controlled substances. Washington State, for example, explicitly allows 30-day non-controlled and 7-day controlled substance emergency supplies when a governor's emergency proclamation covers pharmacy access. The pattern is consistent across most states even when the exact numbers differ, so understanding the framework helps you know what to ask for.

At the federal level, the Emergency Prescription Assistance Program (EPAP) can activate under the Stafford Disaster Relief and Emergency Assistance Act following a presidential disaster declaration. EPAP provides prescription medications, durable medical equipment, and certain medical supplies at no cost to uninsured patients affected by a declared disaster. If you do not have insurance, this program is worth knowing about and registering for during any federally declared disaster event. It does not cover everything and it must be separately activated for each disaster, but it exists to address the medication access gap that uninsured people face after major emergencies.

What all of this means practically: once an emergency is officially declared, go to a pharmacy as soon as you can safely reach one and fill whatever you can. Do not wait until you are nearly out. The emergency provisions exist precisely so that people can top off their supplies when they still have some medication left, not rescue them when they have run out entirely. Combined with the personal supply you maintain in your medication kit, the emergency pharmacy system gives you a meaningful backup layer that most people never think to use.

Know the specific laws in your state before an emergency happens, not during one. Your state board of pharmacy website publishes emergency dispensing rules, and most states update these after major disaster events. Search your state name plus "emergency prescription refill" to find the relevant regulations. Understanding exactly what your pharmacist is permitted to do under your state's emergency provisions means you can ask and confidently when the time comes.

The Physical Kit

The container matters more than most people consider. It needs to be rigid enough to protect the contents from being crushed, sealable enough to keep out moisture and pests, clearly identifiable from the outside, and sized appropriately for its contents without being so large that it becomes inconvenient to grab quickly.

I use a hard-sided waterproof case, the kind sold for electronics or small valuables, with a rubber gasket seal and a latching lid. It is labeled on the outside with a piece of bright tape and a permanent marker: MEDICATIONS and my name. In an emergency where someone else might be helping me, or where I am handing the kit to a family member while I manage something else, the label makes the purpose unambiguous. The case fits comfortably under one arm, which matters when the other arm is carrying the bug out bag.

Inside the case, medications are organized by type and frequency. Daily medications in one compartment, as-needed medications in another, the printed medication list in a waterproof sleeve on top where it is the first thing visible when the case is opened. A small desiccant packet keeps humidity down inside the sealed case. Nothing loose, nothing unlabeled, nothing that requires searching to find. During an emergency, you may be handing this kit to a paramedic, a shelter medical volunteer, or an emergency room nurse who has never seen you before. It should tell them everything they need to know without explanation from you.

Special Medication Considerations

Temperature-sensitive medications present the hardest challenge in this system. Insulin and certain other biologics require refrigeration that obviously cannot be maintained in a standard emergency kit. The solutions are imperfect but real. Insulin cooling cases, which use evaporative cooling or phase-change materials, can maintain appropriate temperatures for 24 to 72 hours without power. For longer emergencies, knowing the location of the nearest facility likely to have refrigeration, whether a hospital, a large hotel with a generator, or a community shelter with power, becomes part of the emergency plan for insulin-dependent individuals. Some insulin formulations are more stable at room temperature than others, and your endocrinologist can advise on which products give you the most flexibility in an emergency.

Epinephrine auto-injectors, carried by people with severe allergies, have their own storage requirements and expiration considerations. Heat accelerates degradation in epinephrine, which can reduce effectiveness exactly when you most need it to work fully. The device should be stored in its original case and protected from direct heat sources. During Milton, the temperature inside my apartment without air conditioning reached levels that would have been problematic for an epinephrine auto-injector stored in an open location. Know the temperature limits of any medication you depend on for acute emergencies and account for those limits in how and where you store it.

Liquid medications require additional packaging protection to prevent breakage and leakage that could contaminate the rest of the kit. Sealed in a small zip-lock bag inside the case, with the bottle protected from impacts by being surrounded by softer items, is the practical approach. Tablet and capsule forms of the same medication are worth requesting from your doctor when they exist, both for storage stability and for the fact that they are easier to transport without breakage risk.

Integrating the Kit Into Your Evacuation Habit

The medication kit only works as an emergency resource if grabbing it is as automatic as grabbing the bug out bag. This requires making it part of your evacuation practice, not just your storage plan. During any evacuation drill or practice scenario, the medication kit comes with you. When you mentally rehearse an evacuation, you see yourself picking up both the bag and the kit. The physical location of the kit should be consistent and obvious enough that you would go to it in the dark, under stress, without having to think about where it is.

Tell anyone who might need to evacuate with you or on your behalf exactly where the kit is and that it comes with the bug out bag. During the Northridge earthquake, the chaos of the first hours meant that people made decisions quickly and without full information. If someone is helping you evacuate and does not know the medication kit exists, it stays behind. A thirty-second conversation in advance prevents that.

The broader principle the medication kit represents is one that applies throughout emergency preparedness: systems that are maintained separately from the main kit, checked on their own schedule, and integrated at the point of use are often more reliable than trying to incorporate everything into one bag. Your medications change more often than your shelter equipment. They have different storage needs. They need more frequent verification. A dedicated system that matches those specific needs serves you better than forcing medications into a general kit cadence that was designed for different items.

Chapter 22: Building Your Kit on a Budget

The Case Against Buying Everything at Once

The bug out bag I carry today represents about thirty years of accumulated gear, replaced items, and lessons learned from things that didn't work. If you added up the retail cost of everything in it right now, the number would be high enough to discourage most people from starting at all. That would be exactly the wrong conclusion to draw.

A functional emergency kit that would have genuinely helped during the Northridge earthquake could have been assembled for well under a hundred dollars. Water, food, a flashlight, basic first aid supplies, a whistle, and a simple bag to carry it in. That kit would have prevented my wife from cutting her feet on broken glass, kept us fed for three days, allowed us to see in the dark, and given us something to signal with. Everything beyond that is refinement, not foundation. Start with the foundation and refine over time.

Priority Tier One: The Immediate Foundation (Under $100)

If you have nothing today and can spend about a hundred dollars this week, this is where every dollar goes. A decent backpack in the 40-liter range, used is fine if it's structurally sound. A case of water bottles plus a package of purification tablets. Three days of calorie-dense shelf-stable food: energy bars, nuts, jerky, and a few freeze-dried meals if budget allows. A reliable LED headlamp with spare batteries. A basic first aid kit that includes bandages, gauze, medical tape, antiseptic, and pain medication. A pealess whistle. A lighter and waterproof matches. A written list of emergency contacts on waterproof paper. Comfortable shoes by the bed.

That list right there handles the most likely outcomes of the most common emergencies. It addresses darkness, thirst, hunger, injury, and the ability to signal for help. You're not prepared for everything, but you're prepared for the scenarios that actually kill unprepared people. That matters more than having premium gear for scenarios that are unlikely.

Priority Tier Two: The Next Three Months ($150–$300)

Once you have the foundation, the next purchases fill the most significant gaps. A quality multi-tool, a Leatherman or equivalent, runs forty to eighty dollars and handles dozens of problems the foundation kit can't. A portable water filter adds a critical purification backup to your tablets. A rain jacket appropriate for your climate. A phone-sized power bank with enough capacity to charge your phone twice. A space blanket or emergency bivvy for shelter. A signal mirror. Basic cash reserve in small bills. A copy of your most important documents.

Spread these purchases over three months and they're easily manageable. Set a standing monthly budget of fifty dollars for emergency preparedness and treat it the same as any other recurring expense. At the end of three months you have a kit that would handle most real-world emergency scenarios with reasonable competence.

Priority Tier Three: Refinement Over Time ($300+)

Everything beyond the first two tiers is genuine improvement rather than gap-filling. A quality hiking pack with a proper frame and hip belt. Better footwear. A canister stove system. A sleeping bag and pad appropriate for your climate. Two-way radios for family communication. A solar charging panel. A weather radio. These are the items that take a functional kit and make it excellent, and they're worth having, but none of them are the items whose absence gets people killed.

Buy tier three items when you encounter them at good prices, when you can test and compare before purchasing, and when your tier one and tier two supplies are fully stocked and maintained. The worst pattern I see in emergency preparedness is people who spend several hundred dollars on impressive gear in one of these categories while having no food, no water purification, and no first aid supplies. That's buying the luxury version of one piece of equipment while leaving the essential pieces empty. Sequence matters.

Where to Buy Without Overpaying

REI member sales happen twice a year and offer genuine discounts on quality outdoor gear. Thrift stores and secondhand outdoor gear shops often carry perfectly functional packs, jackets, and sleeping bags at a fraction of retail cost. The only items I would not buy used are footwear, sleeping bag insulation that might have lost loft, and any item where I can't verify structural integrity, like a pack with questionable strap attachment points.

Dollar stores and discount grocers are legitimately good sources for food rotation items, over-the-counter medications, basic hygiene supplies, and batteries. The batteries may not last as long as premium brands in long-term storage, but they work fine if you rotate them annually. Emergency food staples like rice, beans, oats, and canned goods are almost always cheaper at a discount grocer than at a camping or survival specialty store, and they're identical products.

Avoid buying complete pre-assembled emergency kits from big box stores or online retailers. These kits look complete on the packaging but are almost universally filled with low-quality items that fail under real use. The first aid supplies are often inadequate, the flashlights are dim, the food is unappetizing, and the bag itself is usually cheap enough to fall apart quickly. The money spent on a pre-assembled kit is almost always better spent building your own kit from individually selected components at the same price point.

Chapter 23: Firearms in Emergency Preparedness

Why This Chapter Exists

Most emergency preparedness books avoid this topic entirely, mention it briefly and move on, or treat it as a minor item in a personal security checklist. I think all three approaches are wrong. Firearms are relevant to emergency preparedness in ways that deserve honest, detailed treatment, and the people who are going to include them in their emergency plans deserve better than a paragraph. At the same time, firearms are not the answer to everything and they introduce responsibilities and risks that need to be addressed directly.

I am not going to tell you whether to own a firearm. That decision belongs to you, and it involves your values, your household, your legal situation, and your willingness to invest in the training that responsible ownership requires. What I will do is give you the information to think through that decision clearly and to make good choices if you decide firearms belong in your emergency plan.

I'm not going to share my own relationship with firearms here beyond saying that the decision is deeply personal and varies widely among people I respect who take preparedness seriously. What I can offer is the framework for thinking it through. I went through Hurricane Milton alone, in a building with no power and no security systems. The question of personal security during that kind of extended isolation is real, and a lot of people in that situation think about it. This chapter is for those people.

The Honest Case For and Against

The case for including a firearm in an emergency plan rests on a few specific realities. Disasters degrade the social order in ways that are well-documented. Looting follows major disasters in areas with extended power outages. Law enforcement response times during mass casualty events can stretch from minutes to hours or longer. During the days after the Northridge earthquake, there were neighborhoods where police presence was absent for extended periods and people took matters into their own hands in various directions. A firearm in the hands of a trained, competent owner can provide a deterrent and a last-resort option when help is genuinely not coming.

The honest case against, or at least the honest case for caution, is equally real. A firearm that you are not trained to use under stress is not a safety asset, it is a danger to you and to people around you. Stress degrades fine motor skills and decision-making simultaneously, which are exactly the capacities required to handle a firearm safely in a high-pressure situation. People who have never fired under stress, who have never practiced drawing from a holster, who have never done scenario-based training have an inflated sense of their own capability that the reality of an adrenaline-flooded emergency will not support. An untrained person with a firearm in an emergency creates a risk of unintended discharge, accidental injury to innocent people, and the legal and moral consequences that follow.

The honest bottom line: a firearm belongs in an emergency plan only if the person carrying it is genuinely trained, practices regularly, stores it safely, and has thought through the legal and ethical framework for its use. If those conditions are not met, a firearm adds risk rather than reducing it. Chapter 9 covered non-firearm personal security options that are appropriate for everyone regardless of training level. This chapter is for people who meet or intend to meet the bar for responsible armed preparedness.

Choosing the Right Firearm

The emergency preparedness context shapes firearm selection differently than home defense or sport shooting. You need something reliable, manageable under stress, appropriate for the environments you are likely to operate in, and legal in the jurisdictions you may travel through during an evacuation.

No single firearm is optimal for all of those simultaneously, which is why this is a decision that requires thought rather than just buying whatever someone at a gun counter recommends.

Handguns

A mid-size or compact semi-automatic pistol in 9mm is the most practical choice for most people building an emergency kit. The reasons are practical rather than philosophical. 9mm ammunition is the most widely available caliber in the United States, which matters during extended emergencies when resupply may be needed. Modern 9mm defensive ammunition has closed most of the performance gap with larger calibers while generating less recoil, which improves accuracy under stress. Semi-automatic pistols in this format carry more rounds than revolvers in comparable sizes and reload faster.

Reliability is the primary selection criterion for an emergency firearm, not features, not aesthetics, not what looks impressive. Glock, Smith and Wesson M&P, Sig Sauer P320, and Springfield Armory XD platforms have extensive track records of reliable operation across a wide range of conditions including heat, cold, dust, moisture, and neglect. These are not the only reliable options, but they are proven ones. Whatever you choose, it should be a platform with a documented reliability history and available spare parts and support.

Revolvers deserve mention as an alternative for people who are less technically inclined or who want maximum simplicity. A revolver has fewer moving parts than a semi-automatic, is simpler to operate under stress, and is extremely reliable. The tradeoffs are lower round capacity, slower reloading, and generally larger size for equivalent caliber. For someone who will practice infrequently and wants a firearm that is simple enough to operate reliably despite that, a revolver in .38 Special or .357 Magnum is a legitimate choice.

Long Guns

Long guns, meaning rifles and shotguns, have advantages in terms of power and effective range but significant disadvantages for emergency portability. A rifle or shotgun does not fit in a bug out bag in any practical sense and must be carried separately. This creates logistical complexity and, in some emergency situations, unwanted visibility. That said, long guns are relevant to emergency preparedness in specific contexts.

A 12-gauge pump shotgun is the most versatile long gun for emergency home defense and general-purpose use. It is effective at the distances relevant to home and immediate area defense, ammunition is widely available, and the pump action is reliable across a wide range of ammunition types and conditions. The sound of a pump shotgun being racked is also one of the most universally recognized deterrent sounds in American culture, which has practical value in situations where deterrence rather than actual use is the goal.

Semi-automatic rifles in common calibers like 5.56mm or .308 Winchester offer greater effective range and magazine capacity, which is relevant in rural or wilderness emergency scenarios more than urban ones. Their suitability for emergency preparedness depends heavily on the likely scenarios you are preparing for and the legal environment you operate in. Magazine capacity restrictions and feature-based restrictions vary significantly by state, and any emergency evacuation plan that takes you across state lines needs to account for the legality of the firearm you are carrying in each state you pass through.

Ammunition Selection and Storage

Ammunition for emergency preparedness has two categories: defensive ammunition for your carry load and practice ammunition for training. They serve different purposes and should be selected and stored separately.

Defensive ammunition should be modern hollow-point ammunition from a reputable manufacturer. Federal HST, Speer Gold Dot, Hornady Critical Defense, and Winchester PDX are all well-tested defensive loads with documented performance. The hollow-point design expands on impact and reduces the risk of overpenetration, which matters both for effectiveness and for safety around bystanders. Whatever defensive ammunition you choose, test at least a box through your specific firearm before relying on it, because some firearms are finicky about ammunition and you need to know that before an emergency.

How much ammunition to store is a question with no universally correct answer. A reasonable emergency preparedness baseline for a handgun is enough loaded magazines to fill your carry capacity plus at least two reloads, and a stored supply of 200 to 500 rounds of defensive ammunition and a larger supply of practice ammunition for regular training. This is not a combat load, it is a preparedness reserve appropriate for the scenarios this book addresses.

Ammunition storage requires attention to temperature and humidity. Ammunition stored in hot, humid environments, like an unclimatized Florida garage, degrades faster than ammunition stored in controlled conditions. Keep ammunition in sealed waterproof containers with desiccant packs in a climate-controlled area. Properly stored modern ammunition has a practical shelf life of decades, but improperly stored ammunition can develop corrosion and reliability problems within a few years. Rotate your defensive carry ammunition annually, using the old as practice ammunition and replacing it with fresh.

Training: The Non-Negotiable Requirement

I want to be direct about this because it is the part of firearm ownership that people most often shortchange: owning a firearm without serious, ongoing training is worse than not owning one. The confidence that comes from owning a firearm without the competence to match it is actively dangerous. I have seen this pattern repeatedly, people who own firearms, have never shot under any kind of stress, have never practiced drawing and presenting, have never done scenario-based decision-making, and who have a completely unrealistic picture of their own capability.

The minimum training baseline for someone including a firearm in an emergency kit is a basic firearms safety course, followed by a defensive handgun fundamentals course from a qualified instructor, followed by regular practice at a range at least monthly. The NRA, USCCA, and many independent instructors offer progressive training curricula. Beyond basic competency, force-on-force training using simunitions or airsoft in scenario-based environments is where most people discover the significant gap between static range proficiency and actual defensive competency under stress.

Dry fire practice at home, using a verified unloaded firearm, is one of the most effective and underused training tools available. Trigger control, sight alignment, drawing from a holster, and presenting to a target can all be practiced without ammunition, and the repetitions build the muscle memory that makes competent operation possible under stress. Ten minutes of deliberate dry fire practice three times a week produces measurable improvement faster than a monthly range trip alone.

Safe Storage and Access

Safe storage and quick access are in direct tension with each other, and every responsible firearm owner has to resolve that tension deliberately based on their specific household. A firearm locked in a heavy safe is not accessible in a middle-of-the-night emergency. A firearm left unsecured on a nightstand is accessible to children, house guests, and anyone else who enters the home.

The practical resolution for most emergency preparedness contexts is a quick-access handgun safe, sometimes called a rapid-access safe or biometric safe, that can be opened in seconds by the owner while being secure against children and casual theft. These range from simple push-button keypad models to biometric fingerprint readers. The keypad models are generally more reliable than biometric models, which can fail under stress or with dirty or wet hands. Whatever you choose, practice opening it in the dark, under time pressure, until it is as automatic as unlocking your phone.

Firearms stored in vehicles present additional security concerns. A firearm left in a parked car, even in a locked case, is accessible to anyone who breaks a window. Vehicle thefts targeting firearms are a documented problem. If you keep a firearm in your vehicle as part of your emergency kit, it should be in a lockbox secured to the vehicle frame rather than a portable case that walks away with the thief.

Traveling with firearms during evacuation requires advance planning. Firearms must be unloaded and in a hard-sided locked case for airline travel, with ammunition stored separately. Ground travel requirements vary by state, and some states have specific laws about loaded firearms in vehicles, the definition of "readily accessible," and magazine capacity. If your evacuation route takes you through California, New York, New Jersey, Maryland, or Massachusetts, you need to understand their specific firearm transport laws before you go, not when you are stopped at a roadblock.

Legal Framework and the Use of Force

The legal framework governing defensive use of force varies significantly between states and is the part of firearm ownership that people study least and need most. Florida operates under a Stand Your Ground law, which removes the duty to retreat before using force in self-defense in any place you have a legal right to be. California and many northeastern states do not have equivalent provisions and require that retreat be attempted when possible before deadly force is justified. These are not minor procedural differences, they determine whether a defensive shooting results in criminal charges or not.

The basic standard that applies in all American jurisdictions is that deadly force is justified only when you reasonably believe you face an imminent threat of death or serious bodily harm that cannot be otherwise avoided. Property crimes alone do not meet this standard in most jurisdictions. Someone running away with your belongings does not present an imminent threat of death or serious harm. The legal, moral, and practical calculus of defensive force is something that every firearm owner should understand deeply, which means taking a legal use of force course in addition to technical firearms training.

Concealed carry permits are issued by states and have varying reciprocity agreements. Florida's concealed carry permit is recognized by a large number of other states, but not all. Several states, including California, New York, Illinois, and Hawaii, do not honor any out-of-state permits. If your evacuation plan involves driving through states that do not honor your permit, you need to understand what that means for how you can legally transport your firearm in that state, which may require it to be unloaded, locked, and inaccessible from the passenger compartment.

Firearms Maintenance in Emergency Conditions

A firearm that malfunctions during an emergency is worse than useless because it creates a false sense of security. Firearms require periodic cleaning and lubrication to function reliably, and the frequency depends on the type, how often it is shot, and the environmental conditions it is exposed to.

In Florida's humid environment, surface rust can begin to develop on unprotected steel components within days, especially after storm conditions where salt air is present. Firearms need to be wiped down with a light coat of oil and stored with desiccant in an area with controlled humidity. During extended emergencies when handling a firearm more than usual, clean it at the first opportunity after any significant use. A basic cleaning kit, including a bore brush, cleaning patches, solvent, and a quality gun oil, should be part of your emergency supplies if a firearm is part of your plan. The kit is small, light, and inexpensive.

Malfunction clearing is a basic skill that every firearm owner should practice until it is as automatic as driving a car. The most common semi-automatic malfunctions, a failure to feed, failure to eject, or stovepipe, all have standard clearance drills that take seconds to perform when practiced but can be paralyzing under stress if never rehearsed. Include malfunction clearing in your regular training, not as an afterthought but as a deliberate part of range sessions.

Integrating Firearms into Your Emergency Plan

A firearm in an emergency plan is not a replacement for the other layers of personal security discussed in Chapter 9. Situational awareness, avoidance, and de-escalation remain the first, second, and third lines of response in nearly every scenario. A firearm is a last resort tool for situations where those first lines have failed and there is a genuine, immediate threat to life. Thinking of it as anything else, as a status symbol, as a first response, as a solution to problems that have non-violent solutions, leads to outcomes that are legally, morally, and practically bad.

If you carry a firearm as part of your emergency preparedness, establish clear protocols in advance with any family members or group members who are with you. Who is armed. Where the firearm is stored during travel. What the rules of engagement are within your group. How you communicate about the firearm in public without drawing attention. These conversations are uncomfortable to have and essential to have before an emergency, not during one.

Emergency shelters, including official government-run shelters, typically prohibit firearms on the premises. This is a policy consideration that affects your planning if sheltering in a public facility is a possible outcome of your emergency. Know this in advance and plan accordingly, which may mean having a vehicle-based secure storage option or a private destination that does not have this restriction.

The final word on firearms in emergency preparedness is the same as the final word on every other piece of emergency equipment: tested, trained, maintained, and integrated into a broader plan. A firearm that you have practiced with extensively, that you maintain properly, that you understand legally, and that fits into a thoughtful security plan is a legitimate emergency preparedness tool. A firearm bought on impulse, put in a drawer, and never trained with is a liability. The difference between those two outcomes is entirely under your control.

Appendix: Complete Bug Out Bag Checklist

This appendix is a reference companion to the main guide, not a substitute for it. Every item here is explained in the chapters above, including the reasoning, the tradeoffs, and alternatives to consider based on your situation. Use this list for your initial build and for biannual inventory checks.

The Bag

40–70 liter backpack with internal frame and hip belt. Rain cover. Water-resistant fabric. YKK or equivalent zippers. Fully loaded weight not to exceed 20–25% of body weight.

Water and Hydration

Four 16-oz water bottles (minimum one day supply in bag). Two collapsible water containers 1L each. Water purification tablets (two bottles, 100L capacity). Portable pump or squeeze water filter. UV sterilization pen (optional backup). Water purification drops (small bottle, secondary backup).

Food and Nutrition

Energy bars: 6–9 bars, tested for heat tolerance. Nuts and trail mix: 1–2 lbs. Jerky or other dried protein: 4–8 oz. Instant oatmeal: 3–4 packets. Three MREs or equivalent freeze-dried meals. Hard candy or comfort food items. Instant coffee or tea if caffeine-dependent. Dietary-specific items as required. Small bottle of multivitamins.

Cooking System

Canister stove with piezo igniter. Two small isobutane-propane fuel canisters. 900ml aluminum or titanium pot with lid. Folding windscreen. Long-handled titanium spoon. Folding camp knife. Solid fuel tablets (12) as backup. Lighter plus waterproof matches as ignition redundancy.

Power, Light, and Communication

LED headlamp with red light mode. Spare batteries for headlamp. Small backup LED flashlight. Two keychain lights. Solar lantern. 10,000+ mAh power bank. 20,000+ mAh power bank (main reserve). Solar charging panel (4-panel foldout). Battery-powered AM/FM/NOAA weather radio. Two-way FRS radios (one pair minimum). Car USB charger. All necessary charging cables plus backups. Paper map of local area and likely evacuation routes. Road atlas. Orienteering compass. Phone with offline maps downloaded.

Shelter and Sleep

Three space blankets. Emergency bivvy sack. Lightweight tarp (silnylon, 8x10 or similar). Closed-cell foam sleeping pad (three-quarter length). Sleeping bag liner or lightweight sleeping bag rated for local low temperatures. 50 feet of paracord. Four small carabiners.

Clothing

Broken-in hiking boots or trail shoes. Three pairs wool or synthetic socks. Two wool or synthetic base layer tops. Two wool or synthetic base layer bottoms. One insulating layer (fleece jacket or synthetic puffy). Rain jacket (waterproof-breathable). One backup pair of hiking pants. Leather or cut-resistant work gloves. Wool or fleece knit hat. Sun hat with brim. Lightweight balaclava or neck gaiter. Seasonal additions as appropriate for local climate.

Health and Hygiene

Assorted adhesive bandages in multiple sizes. Gauze pads and medical tape. Elastic bandage (2-inch and 4-inch). Antiseptic wipes and antiseptic solution. Ibuprofen and acetaminophen. Antihistamine (Benadryl). Aspirin. Anti-diarrheal medication. Prescription medications: maintained in separate dedicated medication kit (see Chapter 21), not in this bag. Medical information card (conditions, medications, allergies, contacts). Thermometer. Body wipes (camping or military grade). Travel toothbrush and small toothpaste. Hand sanitizer. Toilet paper. Feminine hygiene products as needed. Foot powder. Sunscreen SPF 30+. Insect repellent. Small mirror. Razor and comb as desired.

Tools and Repair

Quality multi-tool (Leatherman or equivalent). Fixed-blade knife (small, 3–4 inch blade). Knife sharpener. Duct tape (several feet wrapped around water bottle or poles). Electrical tape. Cable ties (20 assorted). Super glue (2 tubes). Wire (small coil, multi-strand). Sewing kit (needles, thread, safety pins). Bungee cords (4). Tarp repair tape. Extra boot laces. Replacement water bottle cap.

Fire Starting

Bic lighter (2). Waterproof matches in waterproof container. Ferro rod with striker. Petroleum jelly-soaked cotton balls in small container. Fire cubes (6). Solid fuel tablets serve dual purpose as backup tinder.

Signaling

Pealess emergency whistle (clipped to bag exterior). Glass signal mirror with sighting hole. Chemical light sticks: 2 green, 2 red. Personal locator beacon (PLB) or satellite messenger if your activities warrant it.

Documentation and Security

Copies of: driver's license/ID, passport, Social Security card, birth certificate, insurance policies, financial account information, medical records and prescription list, property documents, legal documents (will, POA). Emergency contact list on waterproof paper. $500 in small bills, distributed through bag. USB drive with encrypted digital document copies. Medical alert card in wallet. Passwords for critical accounts (secure storage method).

Personal Security

Pepper spray (legal in your jurisdiction). Personal alarm. Tactical pen. Heavy flashlight (dual purpose). Know the laws in areas you may travel through.

Morale and Mental Health

Small book or e-reader loaded with reading material. Deck of cards. Comfort food items beyond emergency rations. Familiar small personal item. Journal and pen. Child-specific comfort items if applicable.

Maintenance Schedule

Every 6 months: Replace all batteries. Rotate food and water. Check expiration dates on medications, purification tablets, sunscreen, and chem lights. Inspect bag and clothing for wear. Update documents and contact information. Test all electronic devices. Every year: Review and update the full kit. Swap seasonal clothing. Replace any item showing structural deterioration. Verify cash supply and replenish if used. Review and update evacuation routes and meeting places.

Conclusion

Every emergency I've been through has taught me the same lesson in a different way. The Northridge earthquake showed me that having supplies and being prepared aren't the same thing. The forest fire on the mountain road showed me that emergencies don't wait for convenient locations. The Christmas hike in the canyon showed me that underestimating a situation is its own kind of emergency. Milton showed me that five days without power, alone, in a building with no security systems, requires a different kind of preparation than any of the physical gear in my bag.

What I've also learned is that people who handle these things well share something that has nothing to do with the quality of their gear. They've thought it through in advance. Not perfectly, not completely, but enough. They know where the bag is. They know what's in it. They've tested the water filter. They've walked the evacuation route at least once in their head. They know who they're calling and in what order if the phones work.

The bag itself is a means, not an end. A fully packed, well-maintained kit sitting in your hall closet changes your actual capabilities only if you've built the habits and knowledge around it. The confidence that matters in an emergency comes from handling the gear, not owning it.

Build the kit in tiers, starting with what actually kills unprepared people: no water, no light, no first aid, no way to signal for help. Get those squared away before spending a dollar on anything else. Add complexity as you develop competence. Rotate your supplies so nothing expires. Practice enough that operating the equipment doesn't require thought.

Customize for your actual situation. My kit in Southern California looked different from my kit in Florida, and both looked different from what someone in Minnesota or Oklahoma should carry. Your climate, your health, your family, your likely evacuation routes are the variables that make your kit yours rather than a generic checklist from a website.

The one thing I'd tell someone just starting out is this: begin today with whatever you have, and build from there. A headlamp, three days of food, a first aid kit, and a full tank of gas puts you ahead of most of your neighbors. That's not cynical, that's just the reality of what most people have done with the information available to them. You're reading this because you've decided to do more.

Your bug out bag is just the beginning of that process of building greater resilience and self-reliance. It's a tool that gives you options when emergencies limit your choices, supplies that sustain you when normal resources aren't available, and confidence that comes from knowing you're prepared for whatever challenges might arise. Build it thoughtfully, maintain it regularly, and practice using it before you need it. Your future self will thank you for the preparation you do today.

About the Author

Richard Lowe brings over four decades of real-world emergency preparedness experience to this complete guide on bug out bag preparation. Unlike many survival writers who theorize from the comfort of their homes, Richard's expertise comes from surviving disasters, extensive wilderness experience, and decades of emergency response training and practice.

Richard's emergency preparedness work began in the mountains and deserts of Southern California during the 1980s, where he developed his foundational outdoor skills through extensive hiking and camping. These early experiences, including several life-threatening situations in remote wilderness areas, taught him the critical importance of proper preparation and the ability to remain calm under pressure.

His preparedness knowledge was tested and refined during major disasters, most notably the devastating 1994 Northridge earthquake that struck Los Angeles. This 6.7 magnitude earthquake provided brutal real-world lessons about emergency timing, family coordination, and the gaps that exist between theoretical preparedness and crisis response. The experience of searching for his missing son while navigating damaged infrastructure and disrupted communication systems shaped his approach to family emergency planning.

Richard's professional background spans multiple industries, giving him unique insights into organizational emergency preparedness and business continuity planning. During his career in the computer industry, he managed disaster recovery procedures for critical business systems, learning how organizations prepare for and respond to various types of emergencies. Later, his work in disaster recovery operations at Trader Joe's provided hands-on experience with large-scale emergency response, supply chain disruption, and the coordination challenges that arise when normal business operations are interrupted by natural disasters.

His formal emergency response training includes completion of Community Emergency Response Team (CERT) certification, where he learned search and rescue techniques, basic medical response, and incident command procedures. This training provided structured knowledge to complement his practical experience and taught him how emergency response systems function during disasters. The CERT program's emphasis on neighbor-helping-neighbor response influenced his community-focused approach to emergency preparedness.

Richard has tested his preparedness knowledge through numerous emergency scenarios, both planned and unplanned. During a major forest fire that trapped him on a mountain road between Lake Arrowhead and San Bernardino, he experienced firsthand how quickly emergency situations can develop and how critical it is to have both supplies and the mental flexibility to adapt when conditions change rapidly. This incident reinforced his belief that emergency preparedness must address psychological resilience as much as physical supplies.

His approach to emergency preparedness emphasizes practical, tested solutions over theoretical perfection. Every recommendation in this book comes from equipment he has personally used, techniques he has practiced, or lessons learned from emergency situations. He believes that emergency preparedness should enhance daily life by providing confidence and peace of mind, instead of consuming it with obsessive worry about unlikely scenarios.

Richard continues to practice and refine his emergency preparedness skills through regular training exercises, community involvement, and ongoing education about new techniques and equipment. He maintains multiple emergency supply caches, conducts regular solo evacuation drills, and stays current with developments in emergency preparedness technology and methodology.

Through this book, Richard shares the hard-won wisdom gained from decades of preparation, practice, and real-world emergency experience. His goal is to help readers develop practical, sustainable emergency preparedness that fits their individual circumstances and local risks, instead of following generic one-size-fits-all approaches that often fail when tested by disasters.

After leaving Trader Joe's, Richard relocated to Florida, where he experienced Hurricane Milton firsthand, riding out the storm alone and managing a five-day power outage that tested every principle in this book. He continues to refine his emergency preparedness practices and help others develop the skills and mindset necessary to handle whatever emergencies life might bring their way.

Books by Richard Lowe

See books by Richard Lowe at
https://masterofworlds.com

Get free publishing insights and industry updates at
https://thewritingking.substack.com

For ghostwriting and book coaching services see
https://thewritingking.com